HOT LEADERS
COOL FACILITATORS
Learning to Lead
One Meeting at a Time

Michael —
Thanks for your interest!,

Brett Wardell

For Harriet Rosenbaum Wendell

HOT LEADERS
COOL FACILITATORS
Learning to Lead
One Meeting at a Time

BART R. WENDELL, PH.D.

Networlding Publishing
222 North Columbus, Chicago, Illinois 60601
visit our website: www.networlding.com

Networlding Publishing
222 North Columbus, Chicago, Illinois 60601
visit our website: www.networlding.com

First Edition, September 2010

Printed in the United States of America

Acknowledgements

It takes profound trust to hand the reins of a meeting, and thus, leadership of one's organization, over to another. I thank the hundreds of leaders who have handed those reins to me. It is through each of you that I learned the secrets of highly effective leadership in real time.

I appreciate the many individuals who encouraged me to write this book. In particular, I offer a heartfelt nod to Ann Muree whose guidance to "just tell the stories," stayed with me during the long hours of writing.

Invaluable suggestions came from readers Jeff Weissglass, Ron Sidman and Roy Plaeger-Brockway; and especially my close colleagues: Bob Kenny, Richard Dowall and Don Weintraub.

I am grateful to David Sibbets, at Grove Consultants, for teaching me how to use graphics in facilitation, and to Don Riso and Russ Hudson, of The Enneagram Institute, for first teaching me about the Enneagram.

Melissa Giovagnoli and John Malysiak at Networlding Publishing helped me to focus the initial manuscript. Lew McCreary, past senior editor at *The Harvard Business Review* provided essential feedback, professional good sense and masterful word-smithing at the midway point. Rebekah L. Fraser contributed her own editorial sensibility and words to the complete manuscript, expertly bringing the ideas of this non-English major across the finish line.

My almost- grown children, Amelia and George, have taught me, and continue showing me, how to use influence with and without authority.

I owe the greatest debt to my wife and best friend, Sandra Whaley, who provided the encouragement, editorial guidance and the design to make this book happen.

TABLE of CONTENTS

Note: *The backbone of this book is the stories that I include to elaborate key points. Every story is based on an actual interaction and event, which I recorded exactly as I remember it unfolding. In most cases I have changed names in order to maintain confidentiality. In some cases, details have been changed or actual events from several interactions have been combined in order to protect my clients' proprietary information, confidential processes and personal privacy.*

–PART ONE–

LEARNING TO LEAD, ONE MEETING AT A TIME

You are a leader...and you don't like meetings. You want to like them, but you don't, and you don't know why. This book will fix that. Meetings—and I'm referring throughout this book to the sorts of gatherings convened to make high-level, bet-the-future business decisions—are often so poorly planned and led that those who attend are rendered bored, passive, frustrated, lethargic, and confused by the end of the first half hour. That's at a merely average bad meeting. The worst, most destructive meetings produce rancor, disunity, demoralization, and business decisions that attendees do not support in thought, word or deed.

I know this because I've spent my career as a hands-on meeting facilitator and executive coach. In this role, I have participated in:

- Industry-first agreements that led to national legislative and regulatory changes for public broadcasting (PBS, NPR & the Corporation for Public Broadcasting)

- The sale of a family-held manufacturing company for $1,000,000,000

- A municipality receiving a superior Moody's bond rating during hard economic times

All of these results came out of meetings in which individuals displayed great leadership.

As facilitator of these and other meetings, I have studied, at close quarters, the crucial elements that make a meeting positive, energetic, and productive, even transforming, as opposed to divisive, depressing, and mysteriously inconclusive. Achieving the former is a complicated blend of art and science. More than anything else, however, it is an act of deft leadership.

Meetings are leadership laboratories, intense microcosms in which the leader's style and substance are on public display. Meetings serve as incubators, auditions, ordeals, showcases, and even Waterloos for leaders of every stripe, from the mildest to the most Machiavellian and macho. The central paradox of meeting leadership and indeed of great leadership in general, is that it calls upon broad sets of skills that rarely, if ever, exist in abundance in any single human being. These skills span the bold action orientation of classic leadership and the cool analysis and perspective of classic facilitation. It's no accident that there's a thriving market for meeting facilitators; the untapped potential of these leaders languishes in the "shadow" of their more dominant portfolio of skills. Yet it's also true that any leader who makes the effort can strengthen his or her deficits and learn to wield the full range of skills effectively, both in and beyond the limited confines of a meeting.

This book is about creating better leaders by showing you how to run better meetings.

Throughout this book, I make little distinction between leaders and facilitators. As I see it, the biggest difference between the two is the length of their contract. Both leadership and facilitation involve responsibility for results. Excuses serve neither, and when no one accepts responsibility for the proceedings or results of a meeting, members of the organization soon suffer as well. If meeting participants can't get into the boardroom because someone has forgotten a key, in the end, it's the leader's responsibility. If the company's pipeline is bleeding oil into the ocean because someone chose to cut corners on equipment, in the end, it's the leaders' responsibility. Great leaders and great facilitators take proactive steps to ensure that each meeting is a success, because they recognize the meeting's power to energize or stall the mission of the organization. Great facilitators are also great leaders. Less-than-great facilitators are not leaders at all.

(Full candor requires this concession: Just as poor leadership some-times yields good results, if only by accident, even a bad meeting can produce a good business decision. Likewise, a positive, well-run meeting will occasionally result in a faulty decision. But good meetings are likeliest to yield good decisions, and bad meetings likeliest to yield bad ones. Moreover, bad decisions that arise from good meetings have a decent chance of being recognized and corrected expeditiously. This is because the responsible parties have, throughout the process, been engaged, empowered, cohesive, and ready to speak their minds—habits that sharpen ongoing management and lead to open, probing inquiry. The bad decisions of inept meetings will play out in a climate of faction-alism and disengagement, with the parties ducking accountability and key players either ill equipped or unmotivated to seek remedies.)

Chapter 1
Wake Up and Lead! Honesty in the Boardroom

There are good reasons why most meetings disappoint.

For starters, the organism consists of people temporarily pulled from their silos and told to behave as a team (they will struggle to leave those silos behind). The participants represent diverse intelligences, egos, temperaments, psychological histories, uneven power dynamics, overt and hidden agendas, etc. In nondescript conference rooms, these elements, fueled by bad coffee, soggy pastry, hard candies, and the intoxicating scent of dry-erase markers, combine to animate the organism. Its soul is most often evident in fluctuating energy and emotional temperatures that swing between cool and hot over the course of a meeting that may last for hours or multiple days.

These temperature shifts can be useful or inconvenient, surprising gifts or sudden threats. Indeed, every important meeting presents moments when the organism can either move in a positive direction or else slip out of control. This can result in damaging disorder and lost opportunity. I've learned this the hard way. Managing a meeting requires incredible alertness. From time to time, I've missed signs pointing to the arrival of a make-or-break moment. Such signs don't flash in helpful neon. Sometimes they merely whisper. The leader and the facilitator must feel the meeting's rhythm, sense the energy in the room, and listen for cues that a breakthrough insight or a festering disagreement could surface.

Timing is everything. Moments that pass unnoticed may never return. Meetings of the kind this book addresses are important enough to deserve the highest levels of skillful leadership and alert facilitation. Such skill develops in leaders who get to know their Standard Operating Temperature (SOT), and their Standard Energy Type (SET), and then go further to explore the shadows of each.

I'll explain Standard Energy Type in Chapter 4. What do I mean by Standard Operating Temperature? As I see it, people operate within a range of temperatures. The "hot" type tends to be more forward, forceful, and driven to rile people up, to see their reaction or get them to take action. The "cool" type generally tries to keep peace, to calm things down, to "chill everyone out." Similarly, I see meetings operating within a range of 'temperatures'. Within meetings, temperature describes the kind of motivation that participants bring to the meeting's goals and each other. Using the temperature metaphor as a guide, a leader can gauge the potential for meeting participants to reach effective decisions that result in the right actions. In other words, the temperature of the room directly affects a meeting's level of success. The leader or facilitator sets the temperature, but anyone in the room can change the meeting temperature either temporarily or permanently.

An Example of Leadership SOT & SET

Throughout my life, and especially in my work, I've been introduced to lots of bold, driven, confident leaders—people who hold and fiercely defend strong opinions, who take decisive action with absolute certainty and no hesitation. My earliest introduction to hot leadership came from my father. His distinctly top-down approach was formed in the military during World War II. My earliest acts of facilitation were to intervene in heated arguments between my father and my older brother. The ability to calm those troubled waters came naturally to me and was the only way to quiet the roiling in my gut.

My basic nature is to be cool, dispassionate, and analytical. I can take pleasure in walking 360 degrees around almost any issue. During the highly polarized Vietnam era, my college classmates and I would debate questions of war, culture, and justice. Much to my friends' consternation, I was able to see positive elements on almost every side. But at some point, deep thinking must give way to decisive action. I was fortunate in my early adulthood to have some experiences that required me to stretch and demonstrate leadership.

In college I was pushed to get off the fence. Because I was a varsity athlete, proponents of the "student strike" (protesting Nixon's invasion of Cambodia) asked me to seek the support of the athletic department. Joined by several others, I made a well-reasoned presentation to what was surely the college's most conservative cadre. Amazingly, they agreed with our position. "Athletic Supporters: Jocks Join Strike," made for a great headline! I had found a way to lead without getting my gut too roiled.

After graduating, I worked as a social studies teacher and coach at the largest public high school in Connecticut. One memorable night, I pulled duty as the sole supervising adult ('adult' at the age of 21) for 250 students rehearsing the class talent show. One of those students, a very large football player whose father happened to be the principal of another school in the system, got in my face over a decision I made about how the rehearsal should be conducted. He did this in a physically intimidating way. Things quickly got tense. Several hundred students watched expectantly. I'm not a big guy—the student had six inches and about 80 pounds on me. But instead of feeling intimidated, I felt angry. I took a deep breath, didn't blink, and told him to back off or I'd call the police. He slowly retreated and took his place with the others. In confronting his threat, I had been clear and decisive; and I had let my anger work for me, not against me. The student could have pounded me to a pulp. And while I'm sure that other students would have immediately come to my defense, I also understood that everyone in the room wanted to see if I had the guts. Frankly, so did I.

I tell this story not to demonstrate any particular courage under pressure, but to share what it taught me. The traits of anger, boldness, and impulsivity, which I had believed were simply alien to me and which I held in some disdain, were actually available for my use as leadership tools in moments when personal or organizational crises threatened. If I was prepared to bring them out of the shadows of my assumed "basic nature," I could develop and control them, like superpowers, for specific valuable purposes.

We are all a mixture of various traits, some present in spades and others only in small concentrations. We tend to be well aware of the dominant ones and not to notice those that dwell in the shadows of who we think we really are. But that doesn't mean we can't bring those shadow traits to the surface and use them. Over the years, I've learned to incorporate my shadow traits into an authentic self that unites both cool and hot leadership skills. Achieving that integration was a journey of a thousand meetings!

Chapter 2
Five Principles of Leadership in Meetings

In the course of my work, I have repeatedly observed the following three phenomena about meetings:

Observation One:
Leaders tend to display incompetence during the very moment they have everyone's attention and hope to perform their best.

Observation Two:
In their desire for control and action, "Hot Leaders" overheat the meeting, creating chaos and forcing participants to make impulsive decisions.

Observation Three:
In their desire to calm conflict, "Cool Leaders" freeze the meeting and end up frustrating and irritating participants.

The balance of this book lays out a framework for leadership that responds to these observations. The material encompasses the core of what I've learned about how to make a meeting succeed. By success, I mean the explicit goals of the meeting were accomplished and the implicit strengths of its leaders were enhanced. I do not mean that every participant was at all times comfortable or on a solid footing; often meetings succeed by causing discomfort before resolving it. A great meeting raises difficult questions and gets at the root of hidden or unacknowledged problems. In the process, a successful meeting will cycle through many temperatures, from very hot to very cool to overheated, and back again.

In the course of developing this framework, I have discovered five principles that play a key role in the fate of every meeting:

Principle #1

Meetings are a reflection of leadership ability. Meetings are an expression of how a leader fosters ideas, creates commitment to the ideas and initiates action. Only great leaders can run great meetings.

Principle #2

Once a leader has convened a meeting, his leadership will never be the same again. Meetings create great opportunities and pose great risks. Meetings either increase influence or destroy it. Even the simplest meeting is not a leadership-neutral activity.

Principle #3

A great leader uses temperature strategically throughout a meeting, to increase the chances that participants will think, connect and act effectively. By virtue of both the heat of his candor and his cool thoughtfulness, the leader builds influence.

Principle #4

A great leader knows himself. Understanding his own up-front leadership type, including the Standard Operating Temperature and Standard Energy Type, allows the leader to recognize and use temperature strategically rather than defaulting to what's automatic.

Principle #5

A great leader does not fear his own shadow. In fact, a great leader will stand bravely in the shadows when necessary, because by allying with the actions and ideas that cause him discomfort, a leader further increases his ability to lead meetings in the optimal range of temperatures.

I am certain you have witnessed these principles in action, but you may not have known what you were seeing. This book will help you recognize, understand, and use the five principles to greatest advantage. In the process, you will become a better leader.

THE MEETING PRINCIPLES IN ACTION:

Principle #1
Meetings are a reflection of leadership ability

Poor leadership creates poor meetings. It's easy to describe a bad meeting because we have all seen so many. Whether it's a management meeting at work, a board meeting at church, or a parent-teacher association meeting, in a bad meeting:

Issues become more confused. People talk too much or too little and get on each other's nerves. People become over-wrought or completely passive, and as a result destroy productive energy. Nothing gets done. Although it's easy to blame a bad meeting on either a hot or a cold temperature setting, the fact is both extremes can stall productivity.

Overly Hot Leaders make each meeting a matter of organizational life and death. They like to talk about "creative destruction"—the process of letting individuals and their domains fail in order to make room for the stronger survivors and newcomers. However, creative destruction in the hands of Hot Leaders becomes simply destruction, as their addiction to heat causes meetings to spontaneously combust. Hot Leaders confuse campfires with spitfires, so instead of inspiring staff, they roast them alive.

Conflict-averse Cold Leaders too often overplay their life-long strength of calming overheated situations. Responding as if every group at every moment were in unbridled conflict, the Cold Leader interrupts each meeting to process the conversation. Consequently, participants lose sight of their reason for being in the room. When Cold Leaders confuse candlelight with forest fires, they fail to inspire staff, and instead extinguish everyone's creative flame.

When it's clear that a leader doesn't know how to regulate the heat, the organization will hire a facilitator to reset the meeting temperature, to create harmony and productivity. Sometimes this works, but sometimes even the facilitator seems at a loss to find the right balance. We've all been in meetings that just drove us nuts. When we finally escape the meeting room, we're either drained or furious. Afterward, it takes time to recover and get back to being effective. Unfortunately, these important gatherings are often where leaders and facilitators put on their best displays of leadership incompetence, aka reality avoidance. We ask ourselves, Why does it have to always be this way? Why do both the facilitator and the boss refuse to acknowledge what's really going on here?

Fortunately, poor leaders aren't the only ones with influence. Great leaders exist, too, and great leaders create great meetings. How does this happen? In a great meeting:

People present eye-opening, energizing ideas and vision. People learn more about each other, and so become more motivated to collaborate. The leader offers direction and support that enables participants to reach decisions, and to follow through on those decisions afterwards. Each participant knows what to do and what not to do to manifest the intentions set forth in the meeting.

A leader demonstrates genuine leadership by stating the truth. Imagine the following summation of a meeting. "Well, I thought we were really going to nail it with this meeting, but you've all done a great job of setting me straight. I thought I knew what was going on, but I didn't really have a clue. I'm not happy and there's no reason I should be. If I'm not able to establish a more honest relationship with you, we're probably all toast."

This is bare-naked, unflinching candor. This kind of honesty energizes people and opens the doors for positive action.

The core competency of a leader is his ability to voice the truth at a temperature that inspires people to put such energy to immediate use. Truth surfaces quickly at some temperatures and not at all at others. In the end, the truth is a leader's legacy, whether he's a Hot Leader or a Cool Leader. Meetings are simply the most effective place for finding the truth within an organization.

Principle #2
Once a leader has convened a meeting, his leadership will never be the same again.

Here is the story of two meetings that changed the way I facilitate; the first was a triumph, and the second was a fall...

Some years ago I accepted the challenge to design and facilitate quarterly meetings that would bring together, for the very first time, the CEO's and board chairs of each of the four national public broadcasting entities: the Public Broadcasting Service, National Public Radio, the Corporation for Public Broadcasting, and America's Public Television Stations. Because these eminences had never before sat in the same room to make decisions, I foresaw some unusual challenges in the participants' lack of familiarity with one another. Moreover, I had learned during prior engagements with public broadcasting stations that there was a history of institutional rivalry, bordering on antagonism, among the four divisions.

"Good luck," various station CEO's warned me, with raised eyebrows.

In the weeks preceding the initial meeting, I spoke personally, and at length, with each attendee. Among them were a former U.S. ambassador, a former state governor, the head of a major foundation, and the founder of what was then the largest Spanish-speaking global television network. Accustomed as these leaders were to having their way, they understood that they needed to influence, rather than dominate, one another in the give and take of a productive meeting. Doing so would be to the benefit of both their individual institutions and the broader community of public broadcasting stakeholders. In part, I expected that my one-on-one conversations would both help me form successful relationships with each leader and tamp down the potential for unproductive hostilities.

The first meeting's goal was simple: to discover whether these individuals had anything to say to one another that could form the basis for future meetings. Would they listen? Could they cool down the hot reflex of conflict, connect with one another, and warm up enough to reach joint decisions? In fact, they rose to the occasion, and an agreement was made to meet quarterly. Guiding principles and ground rules were negotiated, adopted, and faithfully observed. The subsequent meetings were dramatically successful in the decisions the participants reached and implemented. They became an industry fixture, known simply as "The G-4," and continued for years with great success.

I had climbed Mt. Everest. In bringing the four cadres together, I had acted, as circumstances warranted, with either the heat of executive boldness or with cool facilitative calm. Because I was self-aware (**Principle #4**), I was able to put **Principle #3** into action, using temperature strategically, to increase the chances that participants would think, connect and act effectively. I was very proud of myself. Then, several years later, I fell off the summit after missing the signs of a suddenly brewing discontent.

One of the national public broadcasting units had brought on a new, much-heralded and very seasoned CEO. She had been shepherded through the search process by the institution's chairman, with whom I'd developed a close relationship over the course of our quarterly meetings. She arrived for her first G-4 meeting and took a seat beside her chairman. Largely for the new CEO's benefit, I began to review the ground rules that the group had carefully crafted and agreed to as tools for maintaining decorum and focus. The chair interrupted me with the uncharacteristic heat of impatience.

"We don't need those any more," he said. "Let's move on."

Although much more subtle and less menacing than my confrontation with the student years earlier, this interruption from the board chair was in its way a comparable challenge to my role. It caught me off guard, and I failed to respond immediately to the unrecognized change in temperature.

The ride down from the summit was abrupt and bumpy. My churning gut told me that I had done something wrong. I could have turned the moment to the group's advantage by leading everyone in a frank discussion of whether our guidelines were still relevant and useful. Perhaps a consensus would have emerged that we should modify or abandon them, perhaps not. But that discussion might also have brought to the surface the other members' feelings about having a new peer in the room, along with her feelings about joining their club. In the moment, however, I failed to act boldly, and the moment passed. It was the last G-4 meeting I was invited to lead.

Sometimes, "better late than never," simply doesn't apply. Shortly afterwards, I realized that the chair had reacted spontaneously, out of embarrassment in front of his new CEO. Most likely, he suddenly viewed it as infantile that the leaders of the public broadcasting system needed such ground rules to function effectively. I realized in retrospect that what I had missed was a crucial temperature shift. I was doing something that felt coolly pro forma, reciting basic operating principles as a prelude to the heat of real action. However, the chairperson's interruption unexpectedly turned pro forma into the real action. I should have responded by changing my temperature from cool to hot. I should have pressed more boldly to give deeper meaning and value to this seemingly petulant outburst.

What had I learned?

Principle #5
A great leader does not fear his shadow

Everyone has a shadow side. Most of us learn early in life to run from this facet of ourselves. Yet great leaders not only know their shadow, they embrace it. My shadow is heat. I am most comfortable in the cooler regions. However, in this instance, I shied away from my shadow, and temporarily lost my edge. Had I allied with the actions and ideas that caused me discomfort, I could have turned the meeting around.

Great leaders and great facilitators must take the initiative in real time, not in retrospect. To interpret correctly and make the right call in the moment, they need to know themselves thoroughly, both the dominant and the shadow selves, and be prepared to take action informed by this acute self-awareness. Someone like me needs to remember that my roiling gut is a source of important information to which I should pay close attention. A Hot Leader like the board chairman needs to recognize that an energized gut is a necessary-but-not-sufficient component of great leadership. Together, head, heart and gut—cool, warm and hot—are the foundation of great meetings. Had I not let the moment pass, I might have been able to share those lessons with the other leaders in the room! That one not-exactly-pro-forma moment taught me a year's worth of lessons about leadership. Now, when a meeting feels too comfortable, I take that as a signal to ask myself: Is there a truth that the coolness is masking and heat might uncover?

CHAPTER 3
A DIFFERENT WAY OF CONCEPTUALIZING HOW MEETINGS UNFOLD

If you enter the conference room without some picture of how meetings actually unfold, you are wading into a potential morass. Great leaders know what to look and listen for in a meeting. They know how to make sense of the events unfolding before them. A great leader can think on the fly, and knows when to amp things up or slow them down. How can you develop this skill?

Start by understanding and recognizing the three predictable scenarios that play out when meeting participants' energy runs hot to cool.

A meeting's temperature rises when group dynamics intensify and participants move toward taking direct action. This heat is often conducive for reaching resolutions. A meeting cools off when group dynamics become less intense, more befitting contemplation, processing, and experimentation. There is an essential middle energy range, a combination of approaches (to be discussed later) that encourages awareness of and connections with colleagues and with vision and values. Within this optimal temperature range, all participants are more likely to get involved and be productive at a level where they are comfortable.

A meeting that operates within a range of temperatures offers the best opportunity for teamwork to thrive. Think of a meeting's temperature as a measure of the group's existing orientation toward action. Nothing but heat produces 'fire-ready-aim' leaders who effectively and quickly lead people right into the middle of a blazing battle before they realize it. On the other hand, insufficient heat produces a "ready-aim-aim" leadership that trances everyone even as the ship slowly and inevitably sinks below the waves.

Finding the Right Temperature

The right temperature has little to do with the whims or needs of the leader or facilitator and everything to do with the needs of those who will actually do the work. Think of it as the right balance between tension and comfort, a collection of sweet spots, which I call the Engaged Field. A meeting is in the Engaged Field when the energy of either the head or the gut is present along with heart energy. This is when interaction is most likely to produce well-reasoned actions that people care about, and that produce results. It's when everyone can and does say, "We're ready. Let's go!"

In order to produce their best work, people sometimes need to feel the heat that surfaces during debate, or they need the pressure that comes when the meeting leader pushes them. People need room to cool down and think. People need to feel just warm enough to have authentic conversations about how to work together. In the Engaged Field, people truly care about and "buy in" to what happens. Meeting participants lean forward in their seats, and let their best work begin to unfold.

Whether you are a leader with an organization to run, or a facilitator with a meeting to run, you must know how to read and modulate temperature towards this Engaged Field. Leaders need strong intuition, not only to sense a business opportunity, but also to sense when to heat or cool a conversation. Great leaders and great facilitators must be aware that their meeting will need heat to engage and energize people, and cold to help the meeting participants get perspective and analyze decisions.

Often, in their desire for control and action, leaders either mismanage temperature or fail to manage it altogether. This happens across the spectrum of Standard Operating Temperatures. Unbalanced Hot Leaders create chaos and inaction by keeping the flame turned up under the organization's goals regardless of what is going on in the room. Unbalanced Cool Leaders create stagnation by squelching even the most productive heat. Meanwhile, ineffective Hot and Cool Leaders swing so dramatically between the two extremes of temperature that participants in their meetings don't know how to respond. Some meeting attendees will "check out" emotionally. The most proactive will simply leave.

Hot Leaders Burn Others Out

Just like the parent of a newborn, the innovator or founder must always tend to his cause. Yet there is a difference between being effectively persistent and being relentless. For example, a founder's single-mindedness feels overbearing as his organization matures. His urgent questions about the organization's survival seem irrelevant to the new people involved. The founder who does not understand this will find himself constantly replenishing his fire's fuel (employees and board members) as one executive after another gets burnt out and leaves.

Hot Leaders tend to hammer people to respond too quickly. They take an environment that should be fertile for constructive conversation and pound it into one that results in unproductive conflict. Impulsively, they raise the temperature in the room by creating debate rather than encouraging conversation, not realizing that people rarely listen to one another in a debate. A debate is typically a gut-based battle of wills and power masquerading as productive interaction. Hot Leaders focus on subjects too heavily to generate productive results. Seeing the lack of productivity doubles their frustration, so they respond by intensifying their demands.

A Hot Leader In Action
(Joe: Standard Operating Temperature – Scorching)

Joe, the founder and president of a manufacturing firm suffering from high executive turnover, jumped in to interrupt his vice president, a violation of a ground rule set by the group several hours earlier.

"Joe, you are on deck, but Sally is still at bat, per the ground rules."

"I know, but I can't let this go on any longer. She is wrong and she must be corrected."

Sally, a relatively new hire, sat stunned, staring at Joe. I weighed whether to coach her through this in front of the group. On second thought, it was clear that the imbalance of power was too much at the moment to put her up against Joe, even with my help. I reminded myself that one of the goals of the meeting was to resolve issues of employee turnover. Accordingly, it was essential I not get hooked and pulled off track by Joe's provocative and heat-seeking behavior. I decided it was time to label aloud the management issues related to the turnover issue. I would do this by pulling focus away from the substance of the specific disagreement and cooling things down.

I asked Sally, "About how long would it take for you to finish your point?"

"About two minutes," Sally replied.

I turned to Joe in an effort to clarify his intentions. "Joe, are you concerned that Sally is so influential that during those additional two minutes, she could take everyone down a path you could never pull everyone back from? Is she even more influential than you?"

"It's just that it gets me crazy to hear this stuff," Joe said.

"I see that... This seems important. Let's take a break, and Joe, let's you and I huddle."

(The words "Gets me crazy" often signal the need for a temperature change. Hence, I initiated our exit stage left and stepped outside with the overheated owner. He immediately reached for a cigarette.)

I turned to Joe and said in a very matter of fact manner, "If you feel there is a real danger here, then let's suspend the ground rules, I'll get out of the way and you run the meeting until you feel the danger has passed. This is your meeting and you can run it however you feel best."

"No. I want you to run the meeting," he insisted.

"When I run meetings, we go by the ground rules. Do you want to ask the group if they'd like to change the rules so you can interrupt whenever you want?"

"No. I think they'd be pissed."

"Okay, but I'm confused. You have all the authority in this room except what you give me, and you feel you need to stop the meeting we planned, because you couldn't wait two minutes? Why do you have to use your power in such a hot and impulsive fashion? Are you so powerful that even you can't control it?"

"I need to think about that," he said, lighting the cigarette and taking a drag.

"I have a proposal to make."

"Go for it."

"Cool things a bit," I suggested. "Ask the group what they propose you do when you are in the situation similar to the one of a few minutes ago, where you feel you are going to go nuts."

When the meeting reconvened, Joe asked the question. The group said they were okay with his interrupting, on two conditions. Joe needed to let the speaker finish his or her sentence so that Joe would know what he was interrupting; and Joe needed to communicate his intentions clearly. Joe's staff wanted to know whether he was issuing a top-down command, or simply stating his views with characteristic passion, in order to test the waters.

Joe struggled but complied with this new approach. His standard operating temperature seemed based on an erroneous belief that he was responsible for motivating his employees to action, because they couldn't possibly motivate themselves. Further, Joe seemed fearful that when and if anyone showed any initiative, it was a direct challenge to his authority, and therefore detrimental to the goals of the organization. Yet in further meetings, Joe's executives were able to discuss with him how his heated interruptions typified his distorted use of power, and alienated his subordinates, which resulted in higher staff turnover.

Is this to say that hot leadership is never called for? No. This company depended on Joe's 'take-no-prisoners' intensity to push for excellence. However, it is imperative that a leader learns how to recognize the difference between heat as a killer and heat as a mover and shaker. It's a question of timing and of amount. Joe lobbed a flamethrower at Sally, when all she needed was a match. His premature and intense push for action threatened to leave him a leader without followers.

Joe's heat became destructive because it was based on a set of closely held untruths:

• Doing something is always better than doing nothing.

• People do something only when on the hot seat.

• If someone can't stand the (scorching) heat, he shouldn't be here.

• Don't trust anyone unless and until he's passed the hot seat test, every day, more than once.

Welcome to the world of the Hot Leader. In this world, everyone is either prey or predator. How does the Hot Leader know whether someone is predator or prey? He turns up the heat and watches what happens.

The ranting of a Hot Leader leaves a group longing for a facilitator to help bring the meeting to a more reasoned, thoughtful and less Darwinian temperature. People want to clear their heads, get some perspective, and approach things strategically, not as if their survival at that very moment hangs in the balance.

Yet the relationship between people who are either self-designated, or designated by their position to lead a meeting, and facilitators brought in to help an organization pull itself together is not easy at the executive level. Mutual disdain, discomfort and disagreement often mark these two different approaches to leadership.

Why do facilitators' behaviors antagonize so many executives who are themselves asking for the protective 'cooling' a facilitator's intervention can bring?' After all, the facilitator's cause must be to further the productivity of the group. This involves helping the group find the right temperature to get work done. Yet for every Hot Leader, there are at least two Cool Facilitators driving people batty in a different, but equally maddening manner.

Cool Facilitators Chill the Room

In their desire to calm conflict, Cool Facilitators freeze the meeting and end up frustrating and irritating participants. They block the natural rhythm of the conversation before creative tension can build, and snuff any productive conflict by seeking security in too much 'processing'.

How often have you been in a meeting where the facilitator distracted everyone from the work at hand to do 'facilitative exercises?'

How many times have you heard this before? "Let's all just take a deep breath and consider the things you appreciate about the person sitting next to you."

Do such suggestions drive you crazy? How many times, upon hearing those words, have you heard someone mutter: This is a waste of time or, Why can't everyone else just shut up so we can get going???

Sometimes no one wants or needs such calming and cooling activities, because everyone in the room intuitively knows that a certain amount of heat can help initiate action. Most people instinctively don't like too cold any more than too hot.

A Cool Facilitator in Action
(Mick: Standard Operating Temperature – Ice Cold)

Mick, the founder and board chair of a start-up, was a visionary economist whose coolly lucid ideas had served him well in securing successive waves of financing from a venture firm. However, he found himself ineffective at leading his newly convened board members to decisions about the pressing business agenda items. He invited me to a board meeting to see what light I could bring to the situation.

After disposing of administrative items, Mick led the participants' attention to an item of particular importance. "I have compiled a list from each of you concerning what you think we have accomplished thus far on our growth strategy. I have transcribed your lists onto the white board."

In short order, the Board members appeared dazed, drawn, and defeated as they looked at the nearly 50 items. It was an impressive demonstration of how to adjust temperature downwards.

"I'm going to move from left to right, pointing to one list at a time. I would first like to hear feedback from each of you as to whether I have recorded the items accurately after we have moved across the board and validated the accuracy of all the lists."

Only a few board members responded. The room grew quieter, as impossible as that might have seemed a moment earlier. As I watched, I thought of how stage hypnotists ply their craft: In a very flat, cool voice, ask people to attend to so many details at once that their eyes and their minds go cross-eyed. At this point, Mick could have sawed his (imaginary) magician's stage assistant in half and no one would have noticed.

In cool facilitation mode, Mick mistook silence for productive calm. Thus encouraged, Mick really got rolling. "Now, we need to prioritize each of the lists to the planning process. I have multicolored stickers," he began, as he rummaged through a folder.

The attendees, who had already frozen in their seats, stared in horror. All forward movement had ceased, until Craig, one of the venture capital members, practically flew out of his chair. In a disarmingly cool manner he said, "Mick, I don't have time for this. Call me when the planning is farther along." With that, he left the room.

Mick stared at Craig's empty chair, looking confused.

What had happened? Craig bolted because the mind-numbing cold was an intolerable temperature for useful interaction (or even for sitting still). The heated let's-get-to-it gut energy that Craig typically brought to a gathering had been stilled by Mick's sub-zero cerebral temperature. The deep freeze made it impossible for anyone in the room to summon the energy to get their head around all the information that Mick presented. It was too chilled, too remote, and too distant from the work at hand. "Please Lord, deliver us from this misery."

Mick had earned the resentment of everyone in the room by arriving with an agenda completely out of touch with the needs of his board members. He was unaware that adjusting his temperature could foster meaningful conversation. In fact, Mick seemed to believe that the same cool energy that attracted his investors would help him successfully lead his company.

The reality is that great leaders (whether they are designated leaders or hired facilitators) use strategic methods to adjust temperature during team meetings, customer meetings, industry presentations and individual coaching meetings. However, Hot Leaders and Cool Facilitators often resist facing that truth. They would rather stick to their life-long prejudices about optimal operating temperature, than see and feel what people in the room need. Many bosses consider cooling things down to be counterproductive and soft-headed. Many facilitators view heating things as either counter-productive, outside their authority or simply mean-spirited.

Extreme Swings in Temperature

The senior management team of a highly successful consumer products company was in a strategic planning meeting with the president. A hard-driving man, Alan held a vivid picture in his mind of how things should be and he could be very demanding of himself and others. To his credit, he accepted the feedback that his people sometimes felt abused by his push to action. He "heard" that they resented being asked to multi-task beyond their capabilities. Unfortunately, Alan had difficulty knowing when he was doing this, and his staff was not practiced in confronting him when he was on a roll. Even more confusing was his knack for interspersing his outbursts of heat with icily controlled use of Power-Point presentations.

On this particular occasion, the senior management team meeting was proceeding smoothly, with slide after slide of spreadsheets displaying objectives and budget possibilities for each unit for the coming year. As the explicit and implicit work assignments began to pile up, I could

figure a

feel unspoken skepticism and resentment heating up among the team members. No one appeared ready to state the truth about the present situation, so I decided to make my move. I stood up from the table with markers in hand and created figure "a." Silently, I stood next to the easel. Catching everyone's attention, I announced, "The title of this is 'Scheduled Train Wreck.'"

I waited, then Alan spoke up, "So, are we planning to do too much?"

This statement of truth broke the dam. Javier, one of the VPs said, "Alan, you know we always plan on too much. There's the expectations

figure b

that grow out of these budget meetings, there are the phone calls we get from you as the quarter unfolds, there are the keep-the-shop-open problems that arise in the plants, and then there are the customer expectations and emergencies. We can't plan for all these. But we all know that quite a bit of this nice Power-Point will get pushed to the floor as we go along."

Others chimed in and, in controlled tones, described specific instances where this had happened.

I next drew figure "b". "Is it just the way corporations work that there are large signs reminding you to yield to whatever the boss expects, regardless of the expectations of the quarterly budget?" I asked. There was much nodding, including by Alan. I turned to Alan. "What is the next question you would like to ask of your team?"

He took the cue, and summoned the courage to open himself to criticism, "Why don't you tell me to stop when this happens?"

I stood by silently, drawing figure "c" as the conversation unfolded. The members of the team were forthright in citing the perceived risks to planting a stop sign in his path. I kept this stop sign in front of the team for a number of months. I e-mailed figure "c" to the team without any text in the body of the message.

In subsequent meetings, I would unfold the tattered sheet and tape it to the wall, within everyone's view. At key moments in these meetings, I would get up from my seat and stand next to the sign.

In these meetings, my leadership role dictated that I model for Alan and his managers how to cool things down temporarily, not freeze them. I initiated brief 'cooling' pauses by occasionally putting the 'stop' sign in front of the leadership team. This made a significant difference in the team's interaction, and eventual performance. Alan began cooling (rather than freezing) things with enough frequency to create powerful interactions within his team. The team felt the momentary changes in temperature provided just enough space for them to be more truthful, which allowed them to continue to work successfully with Alan. The team's cohesiveness grew.

figure c

Eventually, the leaders of a large publicly traded firm saw the solidity of Alan's management team, cited it and Alan's leadership as primary assets, and purchased the organization. His largely intact team continues to lead the most successful enterprise in its industry.

The Benefits of Varying Temperature: The Maple Tree

Have you ever wondered how maple trees produce the sap that ultimately becomes maple syrup? Sugar maples experience a cascade of temperature changes as the cycle of cold nights and warm days commence during late February and March in New England. This sharpened thermal gradient produces a pumping action that vigorously circulates sap from roots to tree crown and back. Drive a tap into a maple about four feet from the ground and, voila, the sap steadily drips out as if a switch was thrown. Absent this thermal variation the sap practically stops.

In a similar way, each temperature zone tends to pump a particular type of productive energy in meetings, especially when bracketed with contrasting temperatures. The right temperature promotes the type of thinking, or caring required to move people from an issue and opportunity toward action and commitment, and then to the kind of perseverance that marks effective leadership.

CHAPTER 4
STANDARD ENERGY TYPE

Even in the most dry business settings, there are a multitude of things to draw your attention. When you enter a meeting, where do you usually focus?

If you notice:
- Who is holding forth;
- Who is sitting in the power spots;
- Who can be heard over the others; and
- Where the center of action lies,

You are focusing on the action and power in the room.

If you notice:
- Familiar faces;
- Who looks like a potentially great collaborator;
- Who you never want to see again; or
- Who you intend to Google™ as soon as you can open your laptop,

Then your focus is on the people in the room.

If you notice:
- A poster or a power-point slide on the screen;
- A lively conversation about the best way to measure customer satisfaction; or
- A gadget you haven't seen before,

Then you are focusing on the ideas in the room.

Action, people and ideas; these categories reflect the three energies of gut, heart and head. Your Standard Energy Type serves as your home base and determines what in the room is of most immediate interest to you. It also provides the fuel for your focus.

The Three Centers of Energy

If the action and power in the room hold sway over you, you're operating from GUT energy. If you focus on who is in the room, and how you feel about each person, you're operating from HEART energy. If you immediately see the most interesting ideas presented or played out, you're operating from HEAD energy.

These energies, or 'wisdoms,' as they are often referred to in Eastern philosophies, reflect the three different approaches that individuals take to the world: thinking, feeling and instinct/action. Our everyday language often reflects these approaches: "Jim has a cool head for figures." "Bob is a warm guy who speaks from his heart." "Sally is a hot ticket when it comes to timing things. Her gut instincts are very solid." There is an increasingly large body of neuroscience, behavioral science and philosophy about these concepts. For instance, from the neuro-anatomy perspective, these energies parallel the cerebral, limbic and stem portions of the brain. In Eastern medicine, these energies are believed to be located literally in the head, heart and gut, rather than in the parts of the brain related to those areas of the body. Adding credence to this approach is the discovery of startlingly complex neuro-anatomical connections within the digestive system and heart, which support the idea that these anatomical areas are centers of thinking.

One will be more comfortable operating from one of these energy centers. However, everyone is capable of using all three sources of energy.

Locus of Energy	Focus in the Meeting	The Questions Raised by that Focus
Gut	Power and Action	How can this situation be brought under control? When will I have the courage to act?
Heart	Commitment and Collaboration	What do my feelings tell me about what is most important?
Head	Problem-Solving	What is the data? What are the possibilities? What is the best answer? How do I implement that answer?

Locus of Energy	Higher Functioning Supports:	Lower Functioning Brings:
Gut	Action on the agenda and/or the purpose, Determination, Persistence, Transparency, Courage	Others consenting out of fear, Energy without focus, Road Rage and Bullying, Rigidity, Burn Out
Heart	Connection, Commitment, Compassion and Follow-through	People pleasing, Inaction towards the goal, Sub-optimal team composition, Inappropriate push for consensus, Cult-like idolization of founders.
Head	Analysis, Visualization of the future, Integrity and Objectivity	Data porn (addiction to non-relevant facts), Rigidity, Hypercriticality, Energy sapping

Solutions that stimulate all three energies have the greatest chance of success.

The Absence of the Three Energies

Frequently, a leader is faced with a meeting situation in which none of the energies can find any traction and consequently, there is no understanding, no connection, and no action. This commonly happens in the middle of a difficult meeting, and is referred to as the 'failure in the middle.' In business, we hear that, 'every project looks like a failure in the middle.' Artists call it "the throwaway" stage, because it is the point when they are tempted to, or do actually, crumple up their sketch and toss it to the floor in frustration. In the following situation, this 'failure' of energy occurred at the end of the first day of a two-day meeting.

By late fall of 1995, PBS was the second most respected corporate brand in the US. However, it had spent its considerable influence marshaling its members to fight a proposal by Newt Gingrich. The new US House Majority Leader had intended to cut PBS out of the federal budget completely.

The efforts of PBS' member stations against Gingrich's 'zeroing out' policy worked. Phone calls, letters and telegrams had poured into Gingrich's office, convincing him to leave some cash in the pot for public broadcasting. Word came back from Congressman Gingrich's staffers to the leaders of the public broadcasting organizations, "I want just one budget request from all of you."

The possibility of coming up with one request that would address the needs of all public broadcasting stations and affiliates had always been out of reach. In the past, congress would get multitudinous financial requests from the various public broadcasting stations and affiliate groups throughout the country, plus another request for funding from PBS. Although many people within the public broadcasting system had wanted to band together to create one budget proposal for congress, no one had ever been able to reach a consensus to make it happen. There were simply too many differences within the vast system of radio and TV stations. What could a two-person TV station in Fairbanks Alaska and Boston's WGBH, with its thousands of staffers, have in common? We were to find out.

When Gingrich laid the money on the line, saying the only way for stations to get funding was to collaborate and design ONE budget request, he put the stations in a unique position. With no choice but to make it work, and no idea how to do that, representatives from the public broadcasting system called me.

In January 1996, in a downtown Washington DC hotel ballroom, I facilitated a gathering of 50 public TV General Managers and Presidents representing stations across the 50 states. It was scheduled to last 1.5 days. The mood at the start of the meeting was something less than optimistic.

"You know, I hate facilitators," was the greeting I received with the first handshake.

"Yes, I know," I responded. — I was accustomed to hearing this comment about facilitators.

This meeting was successful, as were the scores that followed over a six-year period. And it wasn't simply because consensus was reached for the first time in the history of the industry, which it was. This meeting was a trial of leadership that ultimately increased the influence of all involved. It was successful because the management of riotous swings of meeting temperature strengthened the leadership of the individual station executives with each other, and with the 'Nationals' (PBS, NPR, CPB). It was successful because all who attended achieved what they set out to do, including strengthening public broadcasting's position on Capital Hill.

At the last moments of the first day, a station CEO stood up and said, "If the proposals being discussed here are carried out, I'll see you all in court." This burst of gut energy spiked the temperature of the room and sent the heart energy out the door. A giant sucking sound occurred as all sense of camaraderie and collaboration were nuked. A sense of hopelessness was just beginning to fill the space when, seconds later at the strike of 5 PM, I announced, "Per our agenda, we will stop now and resume tomorrow at 8:30 AM promptly."

Moments later, the staff organizing this event were slumped in various states of misery. "Now what do we do?" They asked in genuine confusion as I sat down to join them. They sensed that the feeling of connection and commitment necessary to achieve their goals had been demolished.

I stepped in. "You have done your jobs. You convened this meeting, set the right agenda, and were truthful about the realities. This is the 'failure in the middle'. Happens every time."

The looked at me, clearly skeptical.

"Wait until tomorrow morning." I continued. "We will soon know where we stand. It is always impossible to know at this moment the way that creative chaos will lead. The good news is, truth was spoken in the meeting, in time for everyone to re-gather them selves for tomorrow. Your task is to keep things warm overnight by getting people talking."

Re-energized by my observation, they reconnected to one another and to the CEO's. They worked the hotel bars and lobbies, keeping the temperature warm enough for the next day's work.

The following morning I entered the meeting room to find the group already sitting, ready to go. On an impulse, I relied on the type of facilitator's cute trick that I usually avoid. Picking up a wad of duct tape that had been left by the audio-visual crew, I tossed it towards no one particular in the group. "Speak your mind and then toss to someone else for their turn. "I pass" is allowed."

The room grew ominously silent as the tape ball fell into the hands of a key player who had spoken very little throughout the entire previous day. I expected him to pass, but he didn't.

"I awoke this morning and the first thing that came to mind was I think we're getting somewhere!" He tossed the tape wad to the next person to speak.

I let out a deep breath, as did most everyone else in the room. The convening organization's management team had displayed leadership the previous evening by relighting the heart energy in the group; we could proceed.

Through divine intervention, several feet of snow kept us all trapped in the hotel. With five minutes to go at the end of day 2 (our adjusted ending point), the participants reached an agreement.

I literally laid myself down on the plush ballroom carpet, exhausted.

Chapter 5
Gut Energy's Heat

The body's strongest area is the core, from abdomen to trunk to upper legs, and this region, also known as the gut, provides the drive to get things done. One who leads from his gut is in the present moment. His focus is on what's happening RIGHT NOW. Someone who leads from the gut expects immediate action and immediate results. In the simplest of terms, as the entrepreneur Seth Godin phrased it, gut energy is all about quenching the physical conditions of being "hungry, scared, selfish, and horny." Those are strong motivations to get moving and improve business!

At its best, gut energy is inspiring. Gut energy infuses a conversation with honesty, and its heat provides one with the courage and persistence to set both pace and direction. A good dose of gut energy in a meeting can get people off the dime by alerting everyone to the reality of the current situation.

At its worst, gut energy dominates a person's thoughts and leads him to dominate others, offering a tin ear to anyone else's realities. In excess, gut energy keeps a person following the proverbial carrot, as the brain screens out incoming data that does not align with the gut's goal. As gut energy builds momentum, it feeds on itself, and pulls everyone in the room towards the increasing heat and away from the other energies. Gut energy has an insatiable appetite.

Abuses of Gut Energy

What happens if there is too much gut energy in the room? Without the moderating effect of the heart, and the cooling effect of the brain, gut energy alone can cause conversation to boil over. Too much gut energy fills the room, stifling the head and the heart. The meeting over-heats. Action is unrestrained by clear understanding and compassion.

When there is too much gut energy, without the moderating influ-ences of the heart and the head, there is also the risk that the meeting will produce a false consensus. People are energized to say something, even if it's impulsive. The room is energized but loses focus. Decision-making competence decreases. The facts get left behind. Participants may become overbearing, polarized or passive-aggressive, saying 'yes' when they mean 'no', just to get the hyper-energized leader off their backs. Things can get really ugly as the meeting boils over into bullying and unrestrained emotion. It's like political conversation devoid of the heart energy of a social contract, or the head energy of collecting data. The result is the paralysis of political gridlock. Think 'road rage.' People begin to think of one another as either prey or predator. People start giving each other the 'virtual finger,' or else, disgusted and fearful, they check out. Much of the public discourse in the U.S. takes place at this energy.

Consider the term 'charette' which is used in the design indus-tries. It comes from the French word for a cart or chariot. Architecture students would work furiously on their presentations even as they rode 'en charette' to their destination (their customer or patron). It also referred to the long carriage rides that government officials would take to reach distant provinces, using the forced environment to hammer out agreements. It has come to mean working under the pressure of the last minute deadline to complete a design. It describes a hot environment; the type of environment Hot Leaders love to create knowing that heat can stir action.

At the same time, remember that an alternate original connotation of 'charette' was the cart used to carry the condemned to the guillotine. The analogy carries forward to the potentially destructive side of the Hot Leader: his tendency to 'make heads roll' in the pursuit of his own goals with a bullying and dismissive approach. Also, when he becomes overheated, he acts thoughtlessly, i.e. as if without his head. The heat generated in the Hot Leader's gut thrusts aside the warmth of heart energy with its concern for others, and the coolness of head energy with its attention to the factual reality of the situation.

HOW TO GENERATE THE HEAT OF GUT ENERGY IN OTHERS

- Model courage in words by speaking forthrightly and candidly
- Model courage in deeds by acting with honesty and transparency
- Model urgency by using no more air time than is necessary and by helping others to participate efficiently
- Publish a written agenda for meetings and state your agenda in one-on-one interactions
- Underline the specific internal and external benefits to meeting deadlines
- Emphasize primarily natural consequences e.g. "Our competitor will be ready to take market share from us in March"

HOW TO EXTINGUISH GUT ENERGY IN OTHERS

- Scare others by taking unnecessary careless risks
- Be hypercritical
- Intimidate by dominating airtime, bullying
- Remove deadlines
- Keep people in the dark about the consequences of their failing to act
- Keep people guessing about everything
- Emphasize only punitive consequences e.g. "You lose your bonus in one week if you don't get moving."
- Be oblivious to your impact on others.

HOW TO KNOW GUT ENERGY IS OPTIMALLY PRESENT

- People are asking the difficult questions and challenging others to be clear, concise, direct and pro-active
- People are initiating conversation and action
- People respond directly to one another, rather than abstractly
- Body language expresses energy, e.g. sitting up or forward, standing, taking notes, speaking clearly with good volume, using bold and expansive arm movements to accompany their words, direct eye contact.
- People pay attention to time and deadlines

Unrestrained Gut Energy in Action

Ad hoc decision-making groups tend to waver between running too hot or too cool. Participants lack the opportunity to experience heart-centered, temperature-moderating connections, typically fostered by physical proximity and prior successful interactions. When teams of people from different organizations must decide how to divvy up a pool of scarce grant monies frayed tempers are par for the course. A meeting of regulators and academics I once led fell into this predictable scenario.

Prior to the meeting, I spoke with all eight participants by phone. Everyone acknowledged the conflict that had been part of the history of this collaborative effort, yet each person expressed cautious optimism that agreement could be reached.

The meeting went swimmingly for the first three hours. I was able to focus on specific issues until the stiff cordiality driven mainly by cool head energy warmed up to inspire more give-and-take. Participants compared notes about past projects and common interests, and expressed hopes for the future. There was a good mix of gut, heart and head in the room. The temperature was moving from easy laughter to sparring and back again. However, Stephanie, a reserved middle-aged woman, actively participated in discussion, but seemed to be well behind the others in terms of the gut and heat she was bringing to the meeting.

It was time for a break. As others filed out of the room, the convener, Wanda, lingered behind to comment on how well the meeting was going. This was a red flag. Where was the, 'bottoming out,' common to potentially contentious meetings? These meetings usually need to have a failure somewhere in the middle as part of their trajectory leading to eventual success. This failure usually takes the form of too much heat or too much cold. With proper guidance, this bottoming out can provide the opportunity for reaching a more effective meeting temperature. Things were going just too well.

"Any reason not to reality-test that observation by sharing it with the others?" I asked.

She agreed, and when the meeting resumed, she waded right in. "I'm thinking that we are doing well together. What do you all think?"

Stephanie, to her credit, spoke right up. "We are doing well, but I think that's because there are some issues we have not yet discussed, even though Bart has asked us in several ways about them. I'm thinking that..." She didn't get to finish.

Lou, a noted scientist who was vigorous in spite of his years, interrupted her, "I'm tired, Stephanie, of your negativism. Whenever we begin to make progress you bring up something or other to impede us. I just won't stand for it." With that, he stood up, red in the face, and began to walk towards Stephanie's side of the table.

I jumped up in front of him just as Stephanie burst into tears and ran from the room. Now it was my turn to become red in the face and meet gut energy with gut energy, though I kept my voice modulated. "Lou, you need to back off."

He froze.

"I'm not going to allow physical confrontations in a meeting," I continued. "You've got to get your act together regardless of how much your anger at Stephanie may be honestly earned. "

Lou returned to his seat, looking sheepish. As I spoke to Lou privately for a moment in a less-heated fashion, I suggested one of the others go out to check on Stephanie. When she returned, she looked drained, but she contained her emotions.

"Stephanie, while you were out I spoke with Lou and made it clear that approaching you in anger would leave you feeling threatened. That's not permissible in any circumstance." I looked towards Lou, and he nodded. "It would seem that there is a particular set of hot buttons for both of you, which cannot be addressed in a group meeting." This time they both nodded.

Like a helicopter, I rose above the provocative content to cool the energy. "What do you all suggest as next steps?"

Adele, one of the other participants, spoke out. "I think that if my office and Wanda's office get together offline, we can come up with proposals based on today's conversation that might be acceptable to all." Everyone agreed this was a reasonable next step. Several of the participants walked with me to the parking lot, wanting to know my thoughts about the meeting.

"We won't know how it went for a while, " I said. That seemed to satisfy them for the moment.

About three weeks later, I called Wanda's office to check in with her. Her assistant connected us. "I'm right this moment meeting in my office with Adele. We're coming along fine with our proposals, so I won't linger on the phone."

What are the leadership lessons here?

1. Look for the strong gut energy in the room. If you don't find it, search it out by honing in on potentially contentious issues. Gut energy that is not found is gut energy that can later surface unexpectedly to abuse all present. There are almost always fault lines, whether previously detected or not, that can predict a future seismic thermal event such as an explosion of gut.

2. Look for the heart energy in the room. Ask about the participants' history of collaboration and emotional connections if any. Ask if there are key individuals missing from the room.

3. Look for head energy in the room to validate that the agenda is the right one for the issues at hand.

4. It is not the boiling over that does the damage, but how the leadership and the group respond to that abuse that counts. In this case, everyone needed awakening to see that the conversation could be initiated, but not completed, in the room.

5. Leading by adjusting temperature often takes bold action. Pulling away from a hot-button issue to let a boil-over cool takes a potent display of gut energy, but one that differs from the abusers' display in that it's connected to the other energies. Notice that as I used my gut energy to confront Lou, I maintained a heart-centered connection. I addressed him directly, personally and in moderated tones. Yet I also expressed empathy for his frustration. In this case, that required I pull on the heart energy of connection by speaking directly to the individuals involved, rather than making general abstract statements.

6. Outbursts of gut energy often come from people whom one would not expect to explode. People most prone to dramatic abuses of gut energy are sometimes those who are the least practiced in using gut energy, in this case, a professorial type who was expert at bringing head energy into the room. Someone who is unaware of the gut's powerful, occasionally loud, impulses is likely to express gut energy awkwardly at best, and aggressively at worst. Lou's gut energy lay within the shadow of his usual style and skills. Because he was unaware of this source of energy within himself, he was as surprised as the rest of us when it burst forth. It leapt out destructively rather than constructively, because it was not under his conscious and strategic control.

To summarize, when gut energy is abused, people can feel attacked, ignored, diminished or betrayed. People stop caring about each other, what others think, and the meeting's ultimate goals. Participation drops off as conversation devolves into sniping and then open conflict. Eventually people check out. The will to act (gut) overpowers sensibility (head) and caring (heart.)

CHAPTER 6
HEAD ENERGY'S COOLNESS

Head energy has a tendency, once activated, to gather momentum and pull the room temperature so far down that the energies of the heart and gut go into hibernation. Facts are addictive for the head type as much as action is addictive to the gut type. People who like ideas often like to collect them. Some people collect stamps, some collect beer cans, but head people like to collect ideas. We've all seen 'data porn' (data valued regardless of it's redeeming value to others or to any productive truth) even if we haven't consciously defined it. Head energy is essential to success, but like gut energy, it is momentum-seeking and can easily take over if not consciously constrained.

Abuses of Head Energy

When the room is cooled by too much head energy, data is chased beyond the point of diminishing returns. Without the heart-felt connection to the cause and the people involved, and the gut-driven courage to act, any understanding brought by the head lacks purpose. Information for it's own sake is a form of self-indulgence; it's data-porn, unrelated to the cause or the issues at hand.

How many meetings have you attended where the leader shared exciting power point presentations like this one: "Here's a spreadsheet showing the number of paper towel rolls used in employee kitchens and bathrooms. Employing an algorithm to compare two-ply and one-ply rolls, we ran usage against benchmarks in the industry over the past 20 years, controlling for the CPI and GNP..." Did you notice the temperature drop to an arctic freeze?

What happens if the temperature freezes? All will to act is sucked from the room, and although the will to escape is strong, you and your colleagues may find you lack the energy (or guts) to do it! Why? All the

How to generate the Coolness of Head Energy in others	How to extinguish Head Energy in others	How to know Head Energy is optimally present
• Model an analytic approach by drawing conclusions based on available data

• Agree on guiding principles/ground rules for effective in-meeting behavior

• Agree on processes for completion before starting a task

• Make the case for investing meeting airtime in thoughtful, unhurried analysis by stating the risks posed by doing otherwise

• Request that individuals pause to write their thoughts out before beginning discussion of a subject

• Model changing your mind based on the discussion | • Create boredom with data porn

• Dominate air time with explanations and responses

• Raise anxiety by creating unnecessary time urgency

• Move the agenda too quickly leaving little time for contemplation

• Become hypercritical or dismissive of ideas generated

• Reward only results and not ideas

• Change nothing in the face of a well-reasoned argument | • Many people are generating new ideas

• Ideas are freely challenged based on logic and data i.e. there are no 'sacred cows' that can't be questioned

• People are returning repeatedly to the data

• Everyone is engaged based on alert body language

• The focus is on ideas rather than personalities

• People are willing to sit in silence while contemplating

• People raise process questions about how conversation will happen, decisions will occur and actions will be implemented |

facts and figures (aka the head stuff) sap the heart and gut energy from the room. People feel irrelevant and subsequently stop caring about the issues and ideas on the table. People go through the motions in order to get the meeting over, all the while wishing that Scotty aboard the Starship Enterprise would just 'beam them up' and out of their lifeless landscape of a meeting.

Want to freeze a meeting? Make a verbal report to a Board that is more than 10 minutes long. Read each power point slide exactly as it appears on the screen, as if people can't read it themselves. Ask for frequent process checks. Endless power points, endless directions, endless manuals, endless budget sheets... Nobody wants to do anything. Nobody cares.

An Abuse Of Head Energy

On the phone, the voice of Margaret, the CEO of the financial services company was strikingly urgent. "Come in as soon as you can. One of our most respected managers just died of a heart attack last night in the locker room after a basketball game."

An hour later, I was in a room with the company's top executives hearing a more detailed account of the events leading up to the manager's sudden death, and the events that followed. Understandably, they looked and sounded numb. Disbelief and shock are common responses to sudden loss. They wanted my counsel on what to do next. I recommended they convene a meeting of the 100 employees in the building. Margaret would start the meeting with a straightforward description of the facts, as she knew them. Next, with my assistance, she would invite anyone who had additional information to report how they came to hear the news. At that point, I would briefly share information about the stages of grief, explaining what to expect in the coming hours and days. We intended to call additional meetings later. This was a solid plan, mixing head, gut and heart.

Once the meeting began, I quickly realized that Margaret's meeting leadership was out of sync with the feelings she had expressed moments earlier. In the executive suite, she had displayed heartfelt confusion and desperation. In front of her employees, both her presence and her words were devoid of emotion. She spoke woodenly, as if she was dictating notes for a lecture in her office, rather than attempting to connect with her audience. It was clear she had gone completely 'into her head' distancing herself from both her heart and her gut.

Margaret's momentary lack of heart energy was apparent in her disinterest in anyone else's experience. Hearing from others in the room was an essential first step in leading her people and company through this crisis. Instead of reaching out to her employees, Margaret described other crises that the company had endured. The content of her words would have been interesting in another setting, but at this time and place, sharing this information served to distance the CEO from everyone else in the room. People began to shift in their seats, and make sideways glances at one another. A few began to cry openly and left the room.

I acted quickly and decisively, from my gut.

"Margaret, I'd like to take some airtime right now. I suggest that anyone who feels tearful should feel free to remain in the room. Tears are perfectly natural at this stage of things and, in fact, keep us in touch with what is on our minds and in our hearts at this moment. Stay if you can. We need everyone's help with this."

Seeing that I had captured the attention of the audience, I continued: "This is an unbelievably tragic event that has just happened. I did not know Mac like you did, but I feel I know him much more just from the obvious impact losing him has had on you all. Margaret, I know you to be a compassionate woman, and others here have confirmed that. I think the most helpful leadership you could provide right now is to simply share the events of the past 15 hours as you have personally experienced them. That may encourage others to share their experience as well, if they wish."

Margaret opened up. Employees stayed to hear her, and then shared their own experiences with the tragedy. This was just the beginning of a series of meetings that served to strengthen the company and Margaret's leadership. Through these meetings, the CEO became more aware than ever of the influence she stood to lose when she defaulted automatically, rather than strategically, to the world of data and facts.

CHAPTER 7
HEART ENERGY'S WARMTH

While gut energy is about action, and head energy is about data and concepts, the energy of the heart is about people and commitment and follow-through. It directs one's attention towards his personal heart-felt emotions and those of others. When the room is frozen with data-obsessed head energy, heart energy motivates each participant to care what others in the room have to say. When the room is overheated with action-obsessed gut energy, heart energy cools and slows everyone enough to hear others' perspectives. This motivating energy speaks to what each person finds meaningful. Gut energy brings drive, and head energy brings fascination, but heart energy is the 'ground zero' for motivation because it allows everyone to draw on his commitment to others and subsequently, to bring his passion to the table.

Oft-replicated studies of bravery and cowardice on the battlefield conducted by military sociologists and social psychologists during WWII, have convincingly demonstrated that it is the commitment to one's "buddies" that motivate. One's desire to stand by his peers is a more powerful incentive than patriotism, fear of consequences for disobedience, fear of disapproval at home, or even hatred of the enemy. A person sticks it out through the most hellacious conditions because he is connected to his peers by some combination of compassion, altruism and self-interest. In the work place, saying someone is a great team player, an expert collaborator, or an invaluable mentor is to say that he is open hearted. He uses his heart's energy to work with others to get things done.

No one can make an effective decision without considering how it will affect others. Leaders who do not care about others do not inspire anyone, do not manifest positive change, and certainly miss the mark in uncovering the truth about their organization and its challenges. Participation and engagement drop off when heart energy leaves the room. If people don't care, the game is over. There may be head energy that provides analysis and perspective. There may be gut energy that gets the work moving. When heart energy is in short supply people sleepwalk, and the organization lacks clear focus and staying power.

Leaders without heart energy make statements like, "You are either with us or against us." A leader who has not inspired the passion of his employees is just someone talking to himself, surrounded by people who are just doin' it for the cash. The employees would just as soon faint dead away and quit if it weren't for paying the mortgage.

Whether it is a leader or an employee, someone who feels he is betraying his heart in his work is more likely to generate ill-conceived,

How to generate the Warmth of Heart energy others	How to extinguish heart energy in others	How to know if heart energy is optimally present
• Model authenticity • Be transparent about heart-felt emotions such as caring, loss, vulnerability, admiration and enthusiasm. • Express genuine gratitude • Introduce non-hostile and even self-deprecating humor • Share personal information i.e. how you came to be in this organization, how you would redo mistakes from the past, hobbies, hometowns, etc. • Raise questions of buy-in and commitment: "Can you truly support this idea or action?" • Raise questions about what people truly value and most desire • Raise questions about how decisions will affect those who aren't in the room	• Focus on task (head and gut) rather than people • Reach decisions without getting full buy-in • Ignore or marginalize the emotions in the room • Initiate arguing • Shut down dialogue • Miss opportunities to empathize	• People are willing to make open and measurable commitments • People are willing to negotiate and/or problem solve in new ways in order to reach consensus rather than make decisions by majority rule • People are volunteering to pitch in across teams and silos • Emotions are being openly expressed without hostility

even erroneous ideas and materials. In addition, that person works ineffectively and unproductively relative to the goals and needs of the organization. Heart energy tends to work in a middle, but relatively narrow band of temperature. It often takes intentional focus to remain in touch with this warm energy. Most people spend more time learning to plot and race their way to the finish than learning to make the journey with an open heart.

The challenge of leadership and facilitation is to help people care about their work; but no one can legislate, order or persuade people to care. A leader can't dictate when or how people open their hearts to the work. Yet an effective leader can navigate a meeting toward the temperature at which participants want to devote themselves to the project or organization.

Do you think enough of others to care about their commitment to the meeting's outcomes? Do you value each person's involvement in choosing and manifesting the goals of your organization? What happens when someone speaks from his or her heart in a meeting? How do you feel when you hear someone say, "Here's what I really believe in"?

Too Much Heart Energy?

There can be times when too much heart is present, resulting in an over-emphasis on commitment and consensus. Ideas and facts are ignored, and results are forgotten when keeping everyone involved is over-prioritized. Truth can take a back seat when people focus solely on what others want and think.

One often finds an excess of heart energy during the transition from founder to professional leader. It takes the form of loyalty that, while admirable and well earned, impedes the forward progress of the organization.

Unrestrained Heart Energy in Action

"Are you ready to herd cats?" I heard behind me. I turned to see Graham, a physically imposing member of the board of an historic preservation organization. I was setting up my materials prior to facilitating their board meeting, and laughed upon hearing the expression.

I have encountered the phrase, 'herding cats,' at easily 80% of the organizations with which I have ever been associated. Almost everyone believes that his or her meetings are more disorganized than any other. Using such terminology is their way of warning me of what's in store, and coaching me in advance (in a Cheshire cat kind of way) for what they're certain will be trouble. Many leaders find it difficult to accept that a facilitator from outside the organization can come in, take charge, and actually succeed where they have failed. Clearly, Graham was one of those leaders who didn't believe I could bridge the gaps that seemed insurmountable to the board members of this organization. In fact, he had probably fought his colleagues when they voted to bring me in to help.

Graham continued in a cool, smooth voice, "In my volunteer work at a prison, I had a specific way I used to work with prisoners on change. Even the guys with 5th grade education could follow it. It always worked."

I didn't ask Graham why his method (linear & heavy on cool head energy) hadn't worked with his colleagues on this particular board of directors. I just smiled and nodded, as he added, "By the way, I need to leave early."

Ah hah. Having been through countless unproductive board meetings, Graham was losing the will to participate. He'd make his appearance and go when he couldn't stand the chaos any longer. Further, Graham was so sure I would fail to "herd the cats"; he didn't want to be around to watch. What else is he saying? I asked myself.

Noting the example of leadership he proffered, I thought of another, deeper explanation. Maybe he's thinking, "Oh, and one other thing I should tell you. All of us in this organization feel like prisoners." People feel imprisoned when they cannot pursue their hearts' deepest desires. I tucked my musings into a mental drawer, being certain to leave it open just a crack, and commenced the strategic planning retreat of the historic preservation organization.

We worked through the first portion of the agenda as I had arranged with the planning committee. I began the conversation by discovering why each of the board members had originally joined the organization, and what kept them going. We drew a 'timeline' depicting the history of the organization. Then I asked them to create a list of their present activities. They were suddenly looking tired immediately after drawing up a list

of all their present activities. What was it about those activities? I quickly glanced at their to-do list, and noted its length.

The previously closed drawer in my head now opened. Graham had talked about 'prisoners'. The board members felt imprisoned by having so many tasks and so few workers to handle those tasks!

I made the decision to alter the agenda, not the ultimate goal, but the way we would get there. I decided to do a very abbreviated version of an environmental analysis in order to metaphorically rescue them from their prison cells. "Now I have an assignment for you," I said. "I'd like each of you to estimate the number of hours you have spent on organization-related tasks during the past 12 months."

The sum-total of their answers was striking to all: 1,300 hours among the eight members present.

"Then what is the most important question to be answered today in the time remaining?" By asking this question, I continued to hover above the action, where I could maintain perspective.

"How to sustain what is clearly not sustainable" was the immediate reply. It came from Graham, who had said he needed to leave early, but stood at the door, observing.

The other board members reeled off their challenges:

"The schools don't have time for local history because of the state-mandated curriculum and testing."

"The Community Preservation Act grant we received leaves people thinking we are all set."

"Town officials know us and have confidence that we can handle things on our own."

"Our buildings look great on the outside so people assume the restorations are complete."

People no longer looked tired. I summed up what I was hearing: "You are the victims of your own success. People contribute their limited time to that which is urgent. You don't look like you need help. To others, it looks like your organization has everything under control."

"That's right," chimed a well-dressed woman, her eyes open wide. "Our problem is like global warming. It's creeping up on us. We're all in our 50's and have no succession plan."

"So here you are," I explained, "highly energetic action-oriented individuals who find yourselves drained, nevertheless. What would you normally do in this situation?"

"Bring in help."

"And....?" I asked.

"We never have paid for help. Jim, Ethel and Louise never believed in paying others to do what we could do with our own hands."

There it was; loyalty to the now-deceased founders. An excess of heart energy was rigidly connecting the current board members to those founders and undermining both their action and thinking energies. I handed the group black, orange and green markers. "You are now going to vote on each item on your list of planned and current activities. A black hash mark is a vote indicating a 'keep the shop open' activity that board members must do through your own labor. Orange is a vote to place the activity in hibernation for one year, and green is a vote to outsource, to pay others to do the work."

There was not a murmur of dissent as I described this last 'green' possibility, in spite of 'by the sweat of our own labor' having been a core value of the organization for every minute of every year of its 50 year existence. I highlighted the import of their acceptance of that 'green' category. Here was the essential element: "What do you think Jim, Ethel or Louise would think if they were still with us?"

"They would be horrified" responded a long-time member. "But that's OK," he continued.

I paused, and made eye contact with every person in the room, including Graham, who still hadn't left. "Is it okay?" I asked.

There was a momentary pause, followed by nodding all around. The voting produced a clear strategic plan. The group would no longer be imprisoned by the operating principles of the Founders. This was big, yet we were out of time. The Board members were energized and ready to keep going. The group was no longer overly mired in heart energy around their late founders. Appealing to what they could actually put their hearts into NOW broke the impasse.

It was a teachable moment, which I could not let pass.

"I have two things to add," I announced in as clear, steady and centered a voice as I could muster. I dove into the core issue, the limited amount of gut energy they possessed to do what needed doing. "We are going to end now as originally planned, because going past your end time is how you continue to burn yourselves out."

Next, I focused on the topic of head energy, "There is a large group of experts out there who will, I bet, volunteer their time to come in and talk to you during the first 30 minutes of every meeting about commercial use, land development, new restoration techniques, you name it".

At that point, having witnessed a new modus operandi for "herding cats," and having seen a resolution to the long-time problems plaguing the historic preservation organization, Graham left to tend to his other pressing commitments.

Relationships with founders can create dysfunction within organizations, when overabundant heart energy engenders loyalty to ideals and methods that no longer serve the organization. The love and respect that people have for the founders traps them, and they fear moving away from their slavish commitment. People can develop neither the heat to get things moving nor the cool perspective to approach things in a new manner. Their loyalty keeps them stuck in a narrow range of simply warm.

A common situation calling for wise leadership is the departure of a founder. As the successor strives to build his credibility and influence, it can create a crisis for the organization. Sometimes the founder emasculates the successor in meetings. Sometimes the successor exiles the founder, and institutional memory and passion disappear. The facilitator's job is to see that neither the founder nor the successor are diminished or run off. In other words, the leadership challenge is to insure that the heart energy in the room, in the form of allegiances to the founder and or to his successor remain in balance with the other heartfelt needs of the organization.

CHAPTER 8
THE ENGAGED FIELD

Considering the undesirable results of meetings that operate at any extreme temperature, it is easy to see that the optimal meeting temperature is somewhere near the middle of the thermostat. I term this the Engaged Field, referring to the amount of engagement one experiences when operating within this state. Are meeting participants successfully tapping their gut energy to get things done? Is heart energy present to support everyone connecting and communicating? Are the participants making the astute observations, assessments, and problem solving that reflect the presence of head energy ?

In the Engaged Field, heart energy is present along with at least one of the other two energies:

Engaged Field = Presence of Heart Energy
+ (Gut Energy and/or Head Energy)

This rarely happens by chance. The head and gut energies gather momentum, so once engaged they want to dominate the agenda and the temperature. In so doing, they chase away the other energies and in particular, heart energy. While heart energy can crowd out both gut and head energy (as just we have just seen in the previous chapter), it generally can disappear in a flash. It is the presence of heart energy with at least one of the other energies that is the key. If your ideas and/or actions have heart, they are for real. Actions and ideas that are heartless are the orphans of meetings, having neither advocate nor champion. Unfortunately and maddeningly, the leader often doesn't see which decisions are orphans until it's too late.

I don't mean to suggest that temperature must be in the Engaged

Field in every minute of a meeting. Nor am I implying that a meeting without the constant presence of strong heart energy is suspect. The truth is, effective work that will look good in the glare of tomorrow's first light will most often occur when the heart accompanies one of the other energies.

Since heart energy is present, the Engaged Field must be akin to the relaxing state of resting in a hammock; right? Actually, in the Engaged Field, one is challenged more than relaxed. In the Engaged Field, one plays bridge or poker rather than 'Old Maid'. The Engaged Field is a brisk walk along a narrow mountain path rather than an easy stroll through a suburban neighborhood. It is a walk in the surf, against crashing waves, rather than a simple stroll down the boardwalk. All of these activities can be fun, relaxing and engaging, but not all of them require such total engagement. One knows he is functioning in the engaged temperature field when he feels not just challenged, but invigorated. When one must rely on more than one of his energies, and more than one set of skills, he is in the Engaged Field.

How can something so heart-centered feel so challenging? Opening one's heart means being vulnerable. Feeling vulnerable in a meeting (or anytime) can be brutal, but it can bring the greatest rewards. To reap such rewards in business, one may challenge oneself to stretch into the Engaged Field, or to enter the state of 'flow'.

Flow and the Engaged Field

There are points in any good meeting where we are 'comfortable'. This is not the 'comfortable' of a luxurious easy chair, but rather that of enticing play. In psychology, this cognitive state is referred to as 'flow.' During flow, our attention turns almost entirely to the present moment and the current task. Time ceases to exist; in retrospect, it passes quickly and unnoticed. Unencumbered by unnecessary worries, not distracted by interior monologue, and not enticed by outside pleasures, one completes work. Most importantly, the individual or group completes the task well, and on time. It is the same set of sensations and perceptions we feel when we are truly at play. Some describe 'flow' as the closest thing to a 'heavenly' state one can experience on earth.

This may explain the particular irritation many feel towards those

Cool Facilitators who seem especially determined to interrupt states of flow. That irritation is not much different from what children feel towards the adults who interrupt their play.

Stretching Into the Engaged Field

The concept of the 'stretch assignment' provides another perspective on the experience of the Engaged Field. Traditionally, when young managers with high potential are identified, corporations give them a stretch assignment, a project or position that is particularly challenging. The assignment has two objectives, both of which involve speeding up a process:

1. To speed up the newbie's professional growth and development or

2. To expose 'fatal flaws' that should remove the person from the list of high potential candidates

An example would be sending your high-flying brand manager to head the brand in Italy, when he speaks no Italian, has difficulty acquiring new languages, and is a new (and first time) parent. (Yes, there is often a touch of sadism in these assignments as well.)

A stretch assignment resembles weight training in the gym. The goal is to build strength by 'working' a wide range of skills up to, but not quite to the point of exhaustion. The assignment must be within one's capabilities, but barely. The 'weight' is supplied by selecting tasks that are of importance to a range of other people and where success or failure will be thus highly apparent as either unfolds. Is a stretch assignment 'comfortable' in an easy-chair sense? Absolutely not. On the other hand, one feels a desirable state of engagement and tension knowing that so much rests on the outcome.

Bringing a meeting into the Engaged Field is like sailing. We are talking about the complexity of interpersonal dynamics here, not a static practice target. A good sailor, even on autopilot, constantly corrects course. The boat doesn't actually follow a straight line to its destination;

rather, it is continuously adjusting course, albeit with frequent small corrections in the hands of a seasoned skipper.

Energy Type	Indicators of excess of energy type	One Can Lead the meeting to the Engaged Field of Energy by
Too much Gut	Impulsive judgments and behaviors i.e. false consensus, rushing to judgment bullying	Pulling back from and cooling the action to consider more thoughtfully the process and the impact on stakeholders
Too much Heart	Implementation shortfalls because of self-absorption with emotions including over-commitment to past ways of doing things	Pulling back and either heating or cooling to identify where loyalties rest, and reality-test the implications of breaking with past loyalties
Too much Head	Brain Freeze: Participants become overwhelmed with data and 'check out'	Focusing in on and heating up the goal of the meeting and what is necessary to accomplish that goal

In sum, the Engaged Field is the "just right" temperature for truthful concluding (ideas), honest committing (people) and strategic movement (action). Head and gut are momentum-gathering energies, i.e. once engaged, these energies want to dominate the agenda. Heart energy does not have that tendency to fill the space but is relatively ephemeral in that it can disappear in a flash.

The challenge of the leader is to establish the optimal meeting temperatures to support the needs of the agenda, while always returning to the Engaged Field at its center.

CHAPTER 9
THE OUTLIERS: THE SUPERSTAR LEADERS WHO ROUTINELY OVERHEAT OR FREEZE THE ROOM

No one living on this planet gets to ignore the laws of physics. We are all bound by gravity, by laws concerning mass, speed and inertia. However, watching a primo ballerino like Nureyev, a leaper like Michael Jordan, or a sprinter like Usain Bolt, we wonder whether the laws that apply to us actually apply to them. They seem to break all conceptions of what is possible and how to achieve success and leadership in their domain.

This is seemingly true for our superstar leaders. In spite of the behavior of the three energies and the temperatures in which they thrive or wilt, a close look at many superstar leaders leaves us with a striking observation— many of them operate at very hot or very cold temperatures, way beyond the Engaged Field. The extreme heat results from and fosters immense drive coming straight from the gut. On the other side of the coin is the coolness that radiates from an intellectually 'brilliant' concept.

Henry Ford is often cited as one such superstar CEO. He had a vision of how to engineer, produce and create a market for a product. His picture of a vertically and horizontally integrated auto company was compellingly complete; from his factory, where he envisioned iron ore going in one end and a black Model T coming out the other side; to his business model that created the very highly paid work force that would serve as the market for his products. In spite of the losses the company incurred in the 1930's and his less-widely admired anti-Semitic and isolationist beliefs, he left an immense fortune and a sustainable international company. There is little question that he had sizable gut energy that drove ideas into action, but he exuded cold rather than heat. He was not a friendly individual. His words were usually unheated, and his actions reflected a very cold, sadistic nature. (Read *The Reckoning* by David Halberstam to learn more about how Ford angrily destroyed the prototype V-8 engine that his son had so proudly built.).

Other Superstar leaders include Walt Disney, Bill Gates, and Sam Walton. Each of these superstar CEO's ran cool at their peak. They rarely operated in the Engaged Field and did not temper their coolness to create balance; they rarely connected with others, or even seemed aware of others except when discussing their products. They were widely known for their brains and either their tempers, their harshness or their neglect of relationships.

On the other end of the spectrum are those CEO's who run large companies into the ground. Dick Fuld (Lehman Brothers), Ken Lay (Enron) and Al Dunlop (Sunbeam) operated at high temperatures and had equal amounts of gut energy as Henry Ford. Boldness, risk-taking, and drive were their specialty. Yet they were like unguided missiles flying past the target opportunities created by visionary ideas. Their gut energy was the kind that burns-out-of-control, toasting organizations and people until what remains is a pile of ashes.

What is the fundamental difference between the best and the worst of the superstar CEO's? The worst CEO's operate at extremes of temperature that, in the long run, undermine their ability to influence and lead. Conversely, the superstar leaders mentioned above engage their head energy in ways the rest of us can't even fathom. In so doing, they manifest transformative innovations and brilliant inventions. Think Model T, Mickey Mouse, and Wal-Mart.

Superstar leaders have a cause and a vision that is magnetic, charismatic and motivating to others. Yet it is their ideas and vision, not the CEO's personally, which capture the hearts, minds and guts of their employees. These ideas are so galvanizing that they take the leadership burden from their owners. How does this work? Despite its origin in the cool region of the head, a brilliant concept is a super nova whose warmth ripples across time and space to touch employees, and enable them to connect around the implementation of the idea. The supernova's heat wave doesn't stop there; once the idea becomes a solid item, event or activity, its warmth spreads further, to inspire customers and fans.

The Supernova in Action

During a stint as an interim CEO of a non-profit, I managed a mild-mannered and very bright 21 year-old who was in charge of information technology. He was eager to please and looking for a cause. One day he approached me requesting a few personal days. He had placed a petition on his personal web site against President George W. Bush's imminent decision to invade Iraq. Within a day he had 250,000 signatures. He needed a few more days to bolster the site to handle all of the traffic. The next day, a *Wall Street Journal* editorial referred to him by name, and the author asked, "Who is this guy, and who's paying him to do this?"

Within weeks, the head of our IT department had resigned to accept an executive position at MoveOn.org. Suddenly, I was watching a business-suited 21-year-old being interviewed on TV. He had no formal knowledge of leadership, and by nature, he was what I term a 'cool thinker'. Yet despite being cool and cerebral, he had an idea that captured many hearts. As a result, a movement coalesced around his idea.

When followers care greatly about an idea, they forgive leaders their derelict or still maturing social skills. Superstar leaders can get by without paying much attention to room temperature. Their work or ideas shine so brightly that followers flock to be involved. People put their hearts into such an idea or performance even when the leader cares only about the job itself. It is the brilliance of their ideas and actions that create a temperature among the followers that is flush with heart warmth.

Sports fans will get up early in the morning to practice a few set shots like Larry, or blind passes like Magic. It is interesting to note that very few stars such as Larry Bird, Magic Johnson or LeBron James go on to demonstrate equally great leadership in other areas of life. Yet the brilliance of their ideas on the court motivates followers, just as the brilliance of the above-mentioned CEO's innovations engenders loyalty. These superstar leaders may be able to get by without considering the temperature they're setting in the room, but most people who want to become great leaders must understand SOT and SET, and learn to use temperature and energy strategically.

Chapter 10
When and How to Bring All Three Energies into the Room

How does one keep the Hot Leaders in the room while occasionally lowering the temperature to encourage processing and creative thought?

I had the honor of being elected to the position of Town Moderator four years after moving into a small New England town and forty-eight years after my predecessor, Dick, first took office. Since only residents of voting age can actually participate in Town Meeting, anyone who grew up in town would have to be about 66 years old to have ever participated in a town meeting led by a moderator other than Dick. He is widely known outside of our town and highly regarded across the Commonwealth of Massachusetts. In short, Dick is no wuss. He is a Hot Leader, direct with his opinions and immediate with his responses.

"Hats OFF!" he would bark at any town member who stood at the microphone to speak. Bear in mind, this is a rural town with a history of farming. Dress is casual and functional, and I have yet to see the balding pates of many of my neighbors, given their fondness for hats. Yet people always did as Dick commanded (though a few would fail to return for future meetings).

Some grumbled about this hat business, so when Dick retired and I took office, I addressed the issue immediately. Aiming to keep enough heat in the room to maintain respectful alertness, without overheating the issue, I said to the assemblage, "As you know, it has been a custom for so many years to remove one's hat when addressing the Town Meeting that many assumed it to be required by town bylaw. In fact it isn't. Accordingly, I will ask you to remove your hat as a courtesy to the Meeting, but if you feel your civil rights are in any way compromised by the request, feel free to ignore it." I have yet to see a hat worn.

Note that I brought all three energies into the proceedings:

1. Gut: I moved quickly to deal with the issue so as not to delay driving towards the more important tasks at hand.

2. Heart: I made reference to the heart-felt attitudes of various individuals in the room

3. Head: I brought a respectful understanding of relevant information regarding bylaws and town tradition.

As soon as my term as Moderator began, I was inundated with requests, most of which fell into two categories: 'fast' or 'medium'. I interpreted these as 'hot' or 'cooler.'

Dick (left) and the author at Dick's retirement event

"You've got to slow things down a bit so that people of all stripes have a chance to speak their minds," said several members of the community.

"Keep those meetings sped up, like Dick does it," others advised. "Can't stand long Town Meetings."

"Don't let everyone speak his piece," was another common request. "We'll never get out of there."

About 125 town members attended the first meeting, including several folks that hadn't been to a Town Meeting since they'd had a run-in (or ducked a run-in) of one sort or another with Dick. I let people know about the requests I had received. "The reality is that no matter what I do, at any given moment at least half of you will be unhappy with the pace. However, in response to the sense of the meeting as I understand it, I will run the meetings a bit more slowly than in the past."

The explanation seemed to appease most of the group, though of course it did little to change anyone's personal preferences. Accordingly, it was not surprising that I would need to lead the proceedings and remain aware of the impatience of the Hot Leaders in the room and their continuing assessment about whether I would turn out to be wimpishly cool and lethargic in contrast to Dick's assertive and often heated leadership.

During one extended period of debate around a motion concerning some town-owned land, Ruth, a physically frail and elderly woman, long committed to serving on a variety of town committees and town posts, raised her hand to speak. There was certainly no need for her to introduce herself; everyone in town knew Ruth. In spite of her advanced age, and her need for a walker to get about, her clarion voice bounced off the walls without the need for a microphone, "This horse has been about dying for some time now and someone ought to shoot it."

This woman knew how to heat things up! Dame Judi Dench herself could not have put it more bluntly or clearly. No one in the audience had the least question about what Ruth expected of me. Of course, being aware of that expectation didn't, and couldn't, mandate my response.

"Ruth, though I'm not licensed by the Commonwealth of Massachusetts to declare this or any other farm or domestic animal alive or dead, I shall do as you suggest after one or two more comments."

The laughter in the audience served to release some of the heated emotion in the room, including the inevitable tension some individuals always feel when they sense two powerful gut-driven forces of leadership about to collide.

Note that I was able to take a strong stand without being rigid. I call this, "setting a rubber fence," as opposed to "drawing a line in the sand", which is a maneuver favored by Hot Leaders. In so doing, I maintained the presence of the three energies in the room to keep the meeting at a productive level.

1. Gut: I recognized and supported her urge to get going.

2. Heart: I maintained connection with her and everyone else in the room using humor, a reliable stand-by that can be a heart-felt and warming means of communication.

3. Head: By providing, even facetiously, some understanding of the limits of my power, I sent the message that information, not just drive to the finish, was an important variable in the room.

Hot Leaders are rarely at rest. They are driven to test themselves and everyone around them to ensure that things are headed in the right direction. Accordingly, it did not surprise me when this push and pull between heat and cool played out again.

Six months later at the next Town Meeting, emotions were cranked to a greater degree by the budget deficit facing the voters. Members of the school board pleaded with those assembled to keep their budget intact, while many others voiced their regret but resolved to recommend budget cuts across the board, for kids and adults alike. One of the ground rules I had set at the start of the meetings was that all amendments to motions were to be submitted to me in writing, even if it meant taking a brief recess of the meeting to do so.

When Dick, the former Town Moderator, offered an amendment, he was characteristically hot in his pursuit. I dropped the temperature, asking, "Dick, can I have that in writing?"

Dick was in no mood for slowing things down to ensure that everyone had a common understanding of his amendment. "C'mon Bart. There's no need for that! It's only a few words."

Everyone watched, and some folks probably were not surprised that we were knocking heads. With both the former leader and the current leader involved, it was bound to happen. In fact, Dick and I had met privately earlier and discussed the possibility that friction might arise between us in a heated town meeting.

"So Dick..." I had said during that conversation, peering directly at him over my lowered eyeglasses, "Do you know what this look is code for?"

"Why no, Bart, I don't," he had replied.

"It means, does your challenge to the Moderator mean you wish to resume duties as Town Moderator?"

"No, no. I've done my turn," he had assured me. "No, definitely not."

Of course, Dick was seated way in the back of the room at this point, so it was tough to use that particular visual cue. Instead, I turned to the citizenry.

"Would you please excuse the past Town Moderator and the current Town Moderator for a moment while we have a candid, though very public, conversation about Town Meeting protocol? You are welcome to listen in." I made this comment with a smile on my face, and it served to lighten the mood. As luck would have it, our brief public discussion helped Dick to see that there was no need for the amendment after all. Again, my leadership challenge was to keep the three energies in the room so the conflict would not boil over and result in an unproductive meeting.

1. Gut: I kept the heated energy present, but moderated it with humor, by essentially saying, "Let's step outside and settle this, everyone's welcome to come and watch."

2. Heart: Inviting everyone to participate by listening and observing served to maintain connection and caring in the room. Taking a break in the meeting would have dissipated the warmth shared by all who cared enough to watch.

3. Head: By taking a moment to process the disagreement, we were able to come to a better understanding of the need for the rule, as well as an idea of how not to over-apply it.

In the end, Dick needed to understand I was in charge, even if I was being a bit too controlling in the reach of my ground rule. I needed to communicate to Dick that he was still a key player in the proceedings. We both came out with our dignity intact, and I maintained a productive meeting temperature.

Chapter 11
When and How to Change Meeting Temperature

It is essential for every great meeting leader to know how and when to change the temperature. To create a truly effective meeting, one must ensure the proceedings stay within the optimal temperature range of the Engaged Field. The quickest way to change temperature is to change the distance of the conversation from the source of heat.

When & How to Generate Heat

When the conversation becomes too cold, too much in people's heads, or strays too far from the organizational issues that inspire and affect meeting participants, it's time to generate some heat. To do this, heartfelt humor and blunt honesty are most reliable and effective. One can also inquire as to how others are doing, or ascertain whether the conversation is resonating. These questions elicit people's gut-felt comments. Most leaders have used these techniques unconsciously. The real competence is to use them knowingly, on a regular basis to keep the energy moving through and about the Engaged Field.

To demonstrate a commitment to moving ahead, focus attention on what needs doing, boldly push people closer to the task, and encourage them to jump into the action. For example, when a leader confronts a board about the implications of a pending strategic decision that ignores a key competitor's rapid growth, honesty is a potent way to generate heat. Honesty and focused attention helps people to find their gut energy and use it, and it inspires everyone to take ownership. It pushes people to interact more intensely with one another, and to engage with the agenda

To warm things up, a leader sometimes needs to confront meeting participants with provocative questions about what's really going on.

Generate heat by asking:

• "John, are you ready to give us the productivity figures NOW?"

• "Sue, what exactly do you think of our progress?"

• "Fran, are we talking to our members enough?
How do you know that?"

How I Turned Up the Heat on Rick

Over the course of a two-day meeting of CEO's in the tech industry, I determined that one individual needed help connecting with the others in the room and with the agenda. It was clear to me that I needed to throw some heat his way to move him from a completely disconnected and cerebral state, to one where his head, gut and heart were all engaged. Without complete engagement, this man would be unable to be a productive participant in the conference.

Rick was a professorial type, thin and a bit gaunt, with piercing eyes and an air of skeptical intensity. It was obvious he was listening intently to every word of the meeting. That was an accomplishment in itself. The topic being discussed was highly technical and detailed. I had to remind myself not to become overly involved in trying to follow all the nuances of the technology, but to keep my attention on the meeting temperature and the progress toward the promised deliverables.

Rick was typing furiously on his notebook computer. E-mails? Minutes? Ideas? After several hours, most of the other thirty-two participants had joined in. Not Rick.

I zoomed in. "Rick, you looked like you were having some thoughts and I wondered if they might be helpful for what we are doing?"

"No, I'm just taking notes," he replied.

I tried adjusting the focus. "Help me out, if you would, with a reality check. Are we on the right subject? Is there something else we should be discussing at this point?"

"No. We're right on course, thanks," he intoned, sort of like the way a shopper responds to the salesperson's hopeful "May I help you," with,

"No, just looking." The truth was obviously not going to be uncovered just yet.

I thanked Rick, and proceeded with the meeting as before. On my mind was the fact that it is very, very unusual for an invited participant in a high-level decision-making meeting to not voice an on-task comment if the right groundwork has been laid. Had I laid this groundwork? Agreement on goal? Check. Ground rules? Check. Discussion of quorum? Management of airtime? Check and check. The temperature was in the productive range as indicated by the number of participants involved in the give-and-take. Yet Rick wasn't buying in.

At the next break, I approached the convener in private. "What don't I know about Rick and this meeting?"

"Rick is a member of a sub-group of firms in the industry who think we should approach this industry standardization in a different manner. They are beginning to divert some of their budget to their own consultants," the convener replied.

"You didn't mention this earlier," I said.

"It didn't occur to me that it was relevant to this meeting."

Another hour of meeting proceeded. Still no participation from Rick, though he was obviously following every word.

At the next break, I collared Rick and turned up the heat. "You haven't joined in and I'm wondering what that's about?"

"I'm an introvert, Bart," Rick said. "I would think someone of your obvious intelligence would have sensed that by now." It was a bit of a hot response, but at least he showed a flash of heart focus by recognizing something about me.

"Rick, I appreciate that, and I respect that you probably find much of the meeting to be repetitive and overly wordy. Not hot enough for you."

"Yes, of course. You get it."

"Well, thanks, but bear with me while I explain why I'm giving you some heat on this," I pressed. "I'm confused. Your being invited here indicates you are a player in this piece of work, but you are choosing to lay low. When someone of your position does this, I assume that there is something unspoken going on in this room, something that is probably quite germane to the success or failure of the decisions made here."

"What are you trying to say?"

"Well, here's how I see my work: My job is to help everyone in the room increase their influence on the ultimate decision reached by exposing truth wherever it may lurk. I can't do that without you participating actively. Your not participating suggests to me that you think your cards are better served by being here but not participating. Maybe in your mind the wrong people are in this room, not the people with real influence to make success happen. Maybe you don't trust a number of your peers here. I want to make your time here as powerful for you as possible. Show me some of your cards and maybe I can be of some help." I couldn't put more heat on him lest he burst into flames.

"Bart, I have a call to make." Rick said, and with that, he walked away. I didn't have a clue about what might result from my giving him some heat.

Rick was late returning to the conference room. He put his cell phone into his pocket as he sat down. Before long, he had a comment.

"I think we're headed down the wrong path. And I'm not the only one who thinks that. Unfortunately, the folks who agree with me couldn't come today. But, let's get real here." After that, the meeting heated up quite nicely. My proverbial flame had finally caught, and produced Rick's engagement with the results of the meeting.

When & How to Cool Things Down

A calm, relaxed setting helps one access their creative, cognitive capabilities. Here one can quiet the inner chatter, what Buddhists call the "monkey mind," in order to hear the inner wisdom rather than the never-ending 'to do' list of swinging limb to limb through the forest canopy.

When emotions are running too high to be productive, or it seems that participants are overwhelmed with the brisk pace of the action, it's time to chill out. To do this, slow the momentum and emotion of the moment with a dose of objectivity and perspective. This requires rising above a conflict rather than remaining embroiled within it. For instance, when a disagreement ensues between the Vice President of Marketing and the Vice President of Sales about who can hire new people, a leader can turn down the heat by saying something like, "Let's pull back for a moment. How would we know if we can hire anyone at all?"

To someone like Alan, the Hot Leader mentioned earlier, this type of response can feel counter-intuitive, and downright scary. For him, the truth is, "Heat produces action; cool produces lethargy." Alan's fear is that if he and his staff sit around cooling their heels, talking, their competitors will get their business. For someone like Alan, heat is reassuring, while cooling down means risking getting caught with his pants down. Hot Leaders often don't realize they are causing a meeting to overheat and often don't care any way, because they see it as the way to get results. Yet true power is found in and by leaders willing to use the full range of the Engaged Field to reach reality-based outcomes.

Shifting Gears to Cool Down

Race-car drivers know that there are times when they can negotiate a particular corner on the racetrack in less time by entering the corner at a slower, more deliberate speed, and then increasing speed through the turn. Similarly, great meeting leaders know that downshifting allows each participant to take a process check and provides everyone the perspective and objectivity that reduces intensity.

Rather than simply pausing, switching gears and slowing the pace of discussion allows time for reflection and sets the stage for divergent points of view to surface. What feels like a detour can often be the quickest route to the finish line; by slowing the discussion, the leader can actually speed the progress of the group.

Pulling Focus to Strategically Adjust Meeting Temperature

To use a film metaphor, pulling focus will provide the necessary perspective on any issue. Zooming In allows a leader to focus on the minute details of an issue. Being under the close examination of a tight lens will probably make participants uncomfortable, but as discussed previously, a little discomfort can be very useful in generating the necessary heat and energy to inspire action. Pulling back allows a leader to gain a broader perspective, to see the issue in its entirety, while also giving meeting participants some breathing room.

Pulling focus requires more than the twisting of a lens. It requires concentration and the ability to see not what one wants to see, but what is actually there. When pulling focus, an astute camera operator will consider a range of issues that may affect the desired outcome on film. Similarly, an astute leader will consider many factors before choosing when and how to either zoom in or pull back to keep his meeting productive and in focus.

The skillful use of pulling focus helps one arrive at the truth in every type of interpersonal interaction by influencing temperatures most conducive to revealing it. Leaders who wish to use temperature and energy strategically develop pulling focus as a core competency.

CHAPTER 12
CREATING THE ENGAGED FIELD

The second of the previously mentioned Public Broadcasting meetings made the internal storms at the first meeting look like child's play. The first meeting had passed the challenge of 'looking like a failure in the middle', but that did not mean the second gathering would skip that step. In fact, the 'failure in the middle' occurs in most meetings that involve making important decisions. Picture another hotel ballroom, high ceilings, chandeliers, distant walls, and fifty CEO's seated in a large 'U'. In front of the room is the set of ground rules established during the first meeting. "You've got to be sh__ting me!" responded one of the CEO's who had been weather-delayed out of the first meeting. Only a few participants heard his comment, but none would have been surprised to hear his sentiment.

At question was the ground rule that locked all agreements from the first meeting in place. This rule was put in place to discourage the tendency to revisit agreements and ignore the sweat-inducing negotiations that created them. Many agreements are based on interlocking concessions. When participants later opt to change some, but not all, facets of such an agreement, it undermines the intricately woven balancing act that enabled its existence in the first place.

Still, decision-making by consensus was essential. These fifty individuals were charged with creating a proposal to "sell" to the roughly one hundred CEO's not in attendance. If those in attendance did not completely agree on the key points raised during this meeting, there was little chance the CEO's of all the other stations would buy in.

Fifty chief executives watched me intently to see what I would do with the authority they had granted me. Would I protect the ground rules they had co-created? I penned a large drawing of a safe on the central easel. Next I drew an arrow pointing into the slot in the top of the safe. There was no arrow coming out. I stood next to the easel, pausing for emphasis, as I pointed to the safe and the arrow.

"Secure within this safe are the decisions from the first Legislative Advisory Group meeting. You will all notice that, based on the ground rule agreed to at that time, decisions go in the safe, but do not come out. Based on this ground rule, I cannot allow you to change the previous decisions unless the members of the group that made the original decisions have no objections."

Drawing a line in the sand is a sure-fire way to heat up a meeting. This meeting was no exception; with my pronouncement, all hell broke loose. The newcomers sputtered in righteous fury since specific aspects of the agreement were difficult to swallow given their stations' particular situations. They pleaded, begged, blustered and glared. I couldn't blame them one bit. The situation was unfair, but there was no way to make the outcome any more fair than it was. My job was to stand my ground and deflect some of the heat from spilling onto other CEO's and thus, impeding any possible collaboration.

When the moment arrived to cool the meeting a bit, I pulled up and away from the core of the debate to help everyone gain perspective. I drew pictures of three different hats, representing the different roles that the participants needed to consider: 'My Station,' 'Licensees Like Me' and 'Public Broadcasting.' "The purpose today is for you to reach consensus on a proposal concerning these three key perspectives," I said.

I reminded those convened that an essential part of their mandate was to ensure their decision would be palatable to the absent CEO's as well as to themselves. First, I asked the group to provide a sense of the meeting as it existed at that moment. Three basic responses emerged, as the CEO's identified three likely approaches to the issues. Along the wall in an open part of the ball room I hung three poster sheets, each with one of the responses. In doing so, I created both mental and physical distance to keep the meeting on the cool side.

Next, I kept things cool by asking each participant to focus inward, on themselves and their needs. " I would like you to consider the response you would support if your only concern were your own station. 'Wearing' that hat, stand in line in front of the sheet displaying that response."

Three parallel lines formed outwards from the wall. Two lines were longer, one shorter. It was time to push the focus ever so slightly in, by asking the CEO's to observe where their colleagues stood. "Let's pause for a moment to allow you each to look at where your fellow stations have positioned themselves. Any observations?" Note that I did not seek opinions at this time, only observations. In this way, I elicited and received calm, non-judgmental responses.

"Differences exist, though the majority of us are in the center or on one end of the spectrum of responses we created," offered one CEO.

"There are differences, though not nearly as large as could be," said another.

And so on.

By spending 30 minutes cooling the temperature of the room, I created space for people to thoughtfully present their viewpoints and hear the perspectives of their peers. It was now time for me to begin strategically generating the heat that would lead to action and agreement.

What did this look like during the Public Broadcasting meeting? First, I grabbed some heart energy by asking everyone to adopt the perspective of another station's CEO. I requested that people don their

'Licensees Like Me' hats, and position themselves in the line labeled with the solution position they supported. About half of the participants moved. People continued repositioning themselves, until the distribution of CEO's primarily focused on one approach. The close 2nd position held almost all the people who were not standing in the first line.

Lastly, people donned their 'Public Broadcasting' hats and realigned until the vast majority were in one line. We were continuing to work in a warm energy zone, focusing simultaneously on ideas, connections to others in the system, and potential for action.

Now was the time to turn up the flame to generate movement towards agreement. Turning to the 10% who were now outliers, I asked, "What would it take for you to join the others in support of the majority position?" From their positions in line, the outliers discussed how the two lines could come to a consensus proposal.

As the scheduled finishing time approached, I focused relentlessly on the participants' toughest issues. "Let's no longer talk about 'Nice-To-Haves' and 'Important-To-Includes'. And let's not talk in favor of anything. Let's not hear about how you feel. I don't want to hear about feelings. Let's only hear about 'Deal-Breakers' ".

I turned to the four station CEO's who remained apart from the majority. "What are the deal-breakers for you? What can you absolutely not accept? I don't want to hear about anything but that." I kept the focus and the heat completely on these four individuals to spur them to action, while keeping the others involved enough and thus warm enough to maintain their connection to what was cooking.

I couldn't let any part of the room go cold during the final stages of cooking up this agreement. I interrupted anyone who wished to raise any other issue unless it was identified as a deal-breaker. "You will only reach this goal by making some difficult decisions, particularly if you still have your station hat on under your Public Broadcasting hat. You may need to remove your station hat completely, and hold it in your hand. I want to hear only proposals that can bring everyone into the tent," I insisted.

Everyone was both tired and grumpy. This was excruciatingly difficult work. We had moved from using scalpels at the leisurely pace of conversation to using hatchets, hammers and, potentially, guillotines under the pressure of the deadline. My intensity simply articulated the truths of the situation. When, at last, everyone in the room stood in the same line, I asked them to return to their seats. They uniformly sank into their seats with a mixture of relief and weariness.

"I have one last question," I said, moving to the center of the group.

All the credibility I had built over this process was on the line, but I mustered their attention. The job had to be completed, and anything but an intense push to keep the room warm enough would leave the job undone.

"You have accomplished something that has never been done before: A consensus proposal for the industry that has a legitimate chance of receiving the support of those not here. That has been very difficult work," I stated.

"However, true consensus has only been achieved if you all support this proposal outside of here, regardless of your personal feelings or your ideas about what is missing, or imperfect. It is not consensus if you discuss the proposal in any fashion that suggests you are not supporting it. It is allowable to say, 'I don't like the proposal and I think it is going to hurt some stations, but it is the best of all possible solutions and we must all support it.' It's not allowable to roll your eyes and make rude hand gestures while claiming to support all of this. I will ask everyone to stand who will 'sell' this proposal regardless of any reservations you may have".

Everyone stood.

Lastly, I redirected their focus to summon the commitment based in heart energy "Now, look around at your peers. You are making a commitment to each other. When peers betray a peer, immeasurable damage is done. If that happens we would have been better never having met because it is better to not promise, than it is to promise and then renege. That has been the history of many non-profit industries, but only you can determine if that will be the history of Public Broadcasting."

Everyone remained standing. There was silence.

"It is 5:00 PM. Congratulations on the work you have done. Thank you."

The meeting was over.

Let's debrief the meeting described above in terms of the three energies.

GUT: The meeting began with a volcanic outburst of heat energy when I drew the line in the sand. The true feelings of betrayal and entitlement needed to be voiced. It was important to provide an opportunity for the honest expression of these feelings. The heat was searing. It was my task as leader to see that the temperature did not stay this high past the point at which others were willing and able to listen and respond productively.

HEAD: After possibly 30 minutes had passed, I moved quickly to cool off the room by leading participants to the world of possibilities, or ideas and consensus proposals that could be created. I used various means to keep the meeting participants away from the hot button issues: breaking the group into smaller groups, keeping close rein on floor debate and discouraging participants from focusing too intently on the difference between positions.

HEART: The room was now cool enough for people to articulate their views. In order to build the heart energy that would produce the commitments necessary to gain consensus, I slowly pushed in to point out the connections between participants in the room. "Look at the CEO's most like you. About what are they most likely to agree? How does that compare with our own hopes?"

GUT: Once the ideas and people pieces of the puzzle were truthfully articulated, I focused on uncovering the truths about what was and was not possible for people to do (the deal-breakers).

HEART: Long-term commitment is the ultimate test of any consensus agreement. I ended by zooming in to reach a warm temperature that would open each participant's heart to the full meaning of a commitment to the consensus and one another.

This meeting could only succeed if people were truthful about their policy positions (head), their willingness to honor their commitments to one another (heart), and their commitment to action (gut). The true test would occur once we all left the room. In that moment, how could I be sure the commitment was solid? For that matter, how can you, in your quest to develop into a great leader, learn to observe, assess, and use the tactical moves necessary to mange the temperatures of head, heart and gut simultaneously?

PART II

TRAVELING THROUGH THE ENGAGED FIELD;
THE JOURNEY TO GREAT LEADERSHIP

Many believe cool facilitation and hot leadership are two independent and self-sufficient stances. It's important to remember that I am not talking about specific technical skills that CEO's or facilitators use to do their daily tasks. Rather I am referring to the indispensable ability to strategically heat or cool a conversation. The best way to achieve this is to remember principle #4 (great leaders are self-aware), and to cultivate this within oneself.

A great leader builds an awareness, familiarity and acceptance of the dormant parts of the self that operate from reflex action rather than conscious action. Personal discovery and self-awareness are a lifetime's work, but the following steps may speed your process in building leadership competency:

1. Identify your upfront leadership type.

2. Identify the 'shadow twins' to your leadership type.

3. Be aware of the three stages of allying one's leadership type with one's shadow.

4. Label reactions that signal the presence of your shadow

5. Know your 'leadership stretch' and 'escape routes.'

The keys to these steps are in the following chapters.

CHAPTER 13
PERSONA—YOUR UPFRONT
LEADERSHIP TYPE

Thus far, we have discussed two types of leaders: Hot Leaders and Cool Facilitators. In fact, seven other types of leaders exist. Each of the nine leadership types is unique because different core beliefs motivate each one's thinking and actions, including the way each type of leader relates to temperature.

The Nine Types of Leadership

A leader is someone who reveals an insight that inspires others to build on that information for the common good. These insights spring

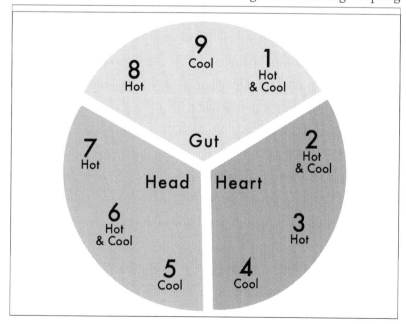

from beliefs central to our type. In addition to beliefs, each of the nine leadership types has an essential question that they (usually silently) ask people.

For instance, the Hot Leader's core belief is I have the strength and the guts to take a stand. The flip side of the belief is the core question the Hot Leader uses to test someone's mettle: do you have the strength to join me in taking action...or not?

The Cool Facilitator's core belief is, I see a harmonious way for us to work together, losing the contribution of no one along the way. The core question for others is, are you strong enough to trust without first having a fight every time?

Each type's motivation is based on such core beliefs and questions; hence, motivation is the most distinguishing factor between types, especially when behaviors look similar. While everyone is guided primarily by the motivation of one particular type, everyone also carries the beliefs, and the motivations, of more than one type to a lesser degree. Step one in your journey toward great leadership, is to identify your dominant leadership style from the Nine Types of Leadership. Remember that each of these leadership types exhibits strengths and shortfalls; no one type is inherently better than another. The ideal leader would be equally adept and flexible at leading in all nine ways.

(The type numbers are provided for ease of identification and grouping by energy type and have no other implication.)

Leader Type Number	Leader Type Name
One	The Hot and Cool Perfecter
Two	The Hot and Cool Provider
Three	The Hot Achiever
Four	The Cool Connector
Five	The Cool Thinker
Six	The Hot and Cool Implementer
Seven	The Hot Innovator
Eight	The Hot Leader
Nine	The Cool Facilitator

Within the nine types are three whose motivations are centered in the mind, three centered in the heart, and three in the gut. When arranged around a circle, one can see that among each of these triplets is a type that operates primarily in the Hot range of temperatures, one in the Cool Range, and one that operates in either range, depending on certain factors that will be explained later.

It may be confusing to see that there are gut-based types that run cool, such as the Cool Facilitator, and Head-based types that run hot, such as the Hot Innovator. Both Hot Leaders and Cool Facilitators are gut-based; yet only one exhibits the heat-seeking, action-oriented behavior on which the gut thrives. That is because for each of the energy centers, Head, Heart and Gut, there is one leadership type that immerses itself in that energy, one type that attempts to constrain and tame it and one type that simply attempts to deny and avoid it. As a result, we see the full range of temperatures within each energy center.

Note to the Reader: The numbers assigned to each type are for ease of identification and are based on historical convention. Be patient with the (out of) order in which I present them in the following tables. It will begin to make sense as you follow along.

The Gut-Centered Leadership Types (Action and Anger*)	Leadership Behaviors	Reflex Behaviors
(8) Hot Leader	• Asserts • Establishes • Controls	• Revels in the heat of action and anger • Uses anger to challenge and learn about others
(9) Cool Facilitator	• Visualizes • Integrates • Facilitates	• Asleep to his anger, • Seeks to cool everyone else's • Seeks meditative activity e.g. exercise, nature, music, gardening
(1) Hot and Cool Perfecter	•Complies, • Improves, • Makes right	• Denies own anger. Active either in following rules or protesting them • Disciplines self to remain cool until heats up to defend what's right

Anger refers to a passion, an urge to make something different, rather than a feeling of rage.

The Heart-Centered Leadership Types (Commitment and Heart's Desire)		
(2) Hot and Cool Provider	• Nurtures, • Cultivates • Sustains	• Denies own heart's desire and commitment to self • Acts with heat on behalf of others but not for himself
(3) Hot Achiever	• Acts, • Overcomes • Wins	• Focuses on outward goals at the expense of inner needs • Becomes a 'doing' rather than a 'being'
(4) Cool Connector	• Feels, • Distinguishes • Creates	• Immerses in heart's desire and commits his heat to his own emotional world • Cool in external actions until he can commit with heart

The Head-Centered Leadership Types (Facts and Anxiety)		
(5) Cool Thinker	• Collects • Categorizes • Solves	• Denies anxiety by coolly collecting facts to analyze and observe • Frugal in commitments
(6) Hot and Cool Implementer	• Commits • Endures • Delivers	• Guided by anxiety: coolly immerses in it or heatedly challenges anxiety directly • Loyal to commitments
(7) Hot Innovator	• Explores • Imagines • Invents	• Ignores anxiety by engaging in interesting activity • Unfocused on commitments

Let's pause to consider further what differentiates each leadership type.

The Heat-Seeking Leaders (3,7,8)

The heat-seeking types, including the Hot Achiever, the Hot Innovator, and the Hot Leader, are the most out-going, action- and future-oriented people. They express themselves in an outwardly assertive, even aggressive manner. They are drawn to novelty and stimuli. Their attitude is, things will happen now that I am here! Their tendency is to charge things up, to spark others in order to understand the possibilities, because their orientation is towards the future, towards influencing, changing or controlling what will happen. It is this drive that produces heat in interaction with others. By the time a meeting is well underway, it will be clear to everyone in the room that the hot types are present and will be active participants. (The one exception is that some Hot Leaders (8) will sit back in order to observe if a meeting is worth their time. More specifically, they often sit back to determine if anyone in the room is strong enough to ally with them in taking charge. Once they have determined the meeting has possibilities, they quickly heat things up.)

Each type of heat-seeking leader has a different motivation for bringing heat into interactions. The heart-centered Hot Achiever believes that by heating things, he will increase productivity, beat the competition and consequently gain the love and acceptance of others. The head-centered Hot Innovator believes that by heating things up, he will inspire others to help him explore the most interesting ideas and possibilities, and eliminate the need to address issues that make him anxious. The gut-centered Hot Leader believes that he must use heat to test others and assert his control over the situation. He believes he is safe when he is in control.

The Cool Leaders (4,5,9)

The Cool Types, including the Cool Connector, Thinker and Facilitator are typically more inward, cautious and watchful. Sometimes called the 'withdrawn types', their first tendency is to pull back from challenges in the belief that things will unfold if only they wait. Their orientation is toward being in the present moment, cooling down heated interactions and slowing the action so they can sense through gut, head, and heart what is happening right now. While they may at first appear to be uninvolved, even 'missing in action', they are actually biding their time before making a move.

Each type of cool-seeking leader has a different motivation for cooling interactions. The head-centered Cool Thinker believes that by pulling back and cooling things down, he can save himself from being drained by the expectations of others or by his own emotional responses, especially anxiety. In this way, he can have the space to actually think clearly and analytically. The heart-centered Cool Connector is motivated to cool things off to create a space to determine what is of most value and how to create loving connected commitments with others about what is most important. Only then will he seek heart-activating warmth. The gut-centered Cool Facilitator is motivated to cool things down in order to create peace and in order to still any chance that potentially destructive anger will erupt.

The Hot and Cool Leaders (1, 2, 6)

Three types, the Hot and Cool Perfecter, Provider and Implementer, can just as easily heat up interactions as cool them down. They are ambivalent about how to act in the face of stimuli and challenges. Sometimes called the 'compliant types', they tend to hang back until they feel they can no longer do so, and then heat up the action as quickly as any of the hot types. Rather than believing things will happen now that I am here, like the hot types, or things will happen if I wait like the cool types, their approach is, things will happen when I earn the right to speak. Their assumption is that keeping their cool in the face of challenges gives them leeway to heat things when it matters most to them.

The overactive conscience of the gut-centered Hot and Cool Perfecter motivates him to keep things cool and avoid any expression of "unjustified" anger. When faced with an unfair situation, the Hot and Cool Perfecter's conscience motivates him to turn up the heat to make things 'right'. The heart-centered Hot and Cool Provider hopes to earn love by meeting others' needs. This motivates him to serve others, and he will only bring heat to a situation if it somehow helps someone else. The head-centered Hot and Cool Implementer is what can go wrong and is worry-prone. Avoiding situations that might increase his anxiety motivates him to operate in the cooler temperatures much of the time.

On occasion, the Hot and Cool Implementer wants to prove that he can shoulder his responsibilities. Generating heat helps him overcome his anxiety and successfully implement based on previous successes.

Have you reviewed the chart of the nine types and discovered you are ALL of them, or (worse) NONE of them? If this doesn't feel right, remember that the hunt is the point. You may be surprised to learn that in itself, the process of 'trying on' each of the types increases the self-awareness and awareness of others that is crucial to effective leadership. Also, note that the categorization of various types as hot or cool does not imply a 'cool' type never acts in a hot (i.e. action oriented) manner, or that a hot type never adopts a cool (i.e. perspective-taking) manner. The information presented about the leadership types is intended to guide and challenge, not prescribe your unique leadership path.

THE NINE LEADERSHIP ENERGIES: THE GUT-BASED LEADERS

One who leads from the gut is innately concerned with issues of drive, power and action. He is constantly assessing who occupies what place on the food chain. Each of the three gut-based leader types deals with these thoughts differently: The Hot Leader (8) attempts to seize it, the Cool Facilitator (9) down plays his own power and tries to tame it in others, and the Hot and Cool Perfecter (1) attempts to subvert his power needs into principles for being 'good' and 'just'.

The Hot Leader (8)

The Hot Leader (8)	Higher Functioning	Lower Functioning
In General	• Bravest of protectors and guardians, constantly searching for others who can be equally as strong • Champion of the vulnerable	• Categorizes others as 'prey' or 'predators' and can become bullying, impulsive and irrational. • Controls everyone and everything but his own impulses
In Meetings	• Stimulates honest conversation and immediate productive action • Empowers.	• Stifles participation with offensive bluntness and impatience with others' need for process • Gets into power struggles (and always wins, in the short run).

Examples: M.L. King Jr., Donald Trump, Lee Iacocca, Rupert Murdock, Pablo Picasso, Ernest Hemingway Saddam Hussein, LBJ, John McCain, Golda Meir

The Hot Leader is a battler, a top gun, an impact player who embraces the energy of his gut. He favors the direct expression of will and action over delay. He believes the best way to know the future is to invent one, NOW. He does not accept delayed gratification, and will happily play the role of 'bad boy' if it means getting what he wants. The Hot Leader is the 'captain of industry' sprawled comfortably upon his Harley Davidson, cigar askew. The term, "My way or the highway" was undoubtedly coined by a Hot Leader. He may not be able to see any other road.

Constantly prepped for a fight with the enemy, the Hot Leader must continually test everyone's mettle. He prefers operating at high temperatures, and will seek heat from numerous exterior sources, like cigarettes, cigars, machinery, the sun or friction-filled relationships. His secret is that he learns through heat and through the friction of pushing and being pushed, and he responds best to those who can hold their ground. Others often misunderstand his heated intentions: the Hot Leader doesn't mean to pick a fight. He just wants to find the truth, which he seeks, naturally, through heat

The Hot Leader can also be a courageous defender of what is right and true. In a time of danger, a healthy Hot Leader is a welcome ally.

The Cool Facilitator (9)

The Cool Facilitator is a diplomat and an integrator, both buoyed and

The Cool Facilitator (8)	Higher Functioning	Lower Functioning
In General	• Powerfully creative and energetic peace-maker and integrator	• Slothful and disengaged towards any inner principles or inner agenda other than maintaining some sense of inner calm through the avoidance of conflict
In Meetings	• Pushes for everyone's participation and towards ultimate agreement • Systematically helps the group through obstacles of conflict, anxiety, nearsightedness and the tendency to keep score of winners and losers	• Blocks deliverables by being overly process-oriented • Seeks harmony where none exists • Talks too much and trances everyone into lethargy

Examples: The Dali Lama, Ronald Reagan, Walt Disney, Abraham Lincoln, George W. Bush, Gerald Ford, Barack Obama burdened by his ability to see all sides of a situation. At ease with others, the Cool Facilitator is a master of bringing simplicity and order to chaos. A champion of context, the Cool Facilitator will always know what to say, provided he has time to get a 'sense' of the surroundings. He uses gut intuition as his guide, so if he is expected to lead without listening to his intuition, he can be caught off guard. With his easy, non-judgmental manner, and willingness to allow the future to unfold organically, the Cool Facilitator brings a calming effect to everyone in his presence. He is eager to find the best in the here and now. He is also ambivalent about wielding power, and can at times implode in self-criticism. At other times, to the surprise of all around him, the Cool Facilitator can explode outwardly in long-denied anger or at least, stubbornness. He will often hang back until asked to participate. This leadership type often prefers to receive an invitation, rather than to assert himself independently.

The Hot and Cool Perfecter (1)

The Cool and Hot Perfecter is driven by two factors: a wish to comply with and stand up for principles of fairness and civility, and a constant awareness of how anything can be made better, even perfected. With a crisp presentation style, the Perfecter is most comfortable bringing order to chaos. Yet this leader can be ambivalent about exerting his power directly. He prefers to earn the right to speak up by being the dutiful 'good guy' rather than the rebellious Hot Leader's 'bad boy'. The Perfecter's chronic dissatisfaction with himself can motivate him to overcome his innate aversion to breaking rules. At such times, the Hot and Cool Perfecter's drive to fix things can heat up and inspire a room or a country.

Cool & Hot Perfecter (1)	Higher Functioning	Lower Functioning
In General:	• Gutsy and relentless in championing for what is right	• Irritatingly judgmental and even sadistic nitpicker
In Meetings:	•Brings intellectual rigor and clarity to planning and discussion	• Becomes mired in details • Subtly and rigidly rejects new ideas • Has difficulty improvising on the run

Examples: Hillary Clinton, Ralph Nader, George Washington, Martha Stewart

THE NINE LEADERSHIP ENERGIES: THE HEART BASED LEADERS

These leaders are innately-concerned with issues of connecting with others, either by impressing others through achievements (3), finding common ground in the world of emotions (4) or establishing connection by being 'in service' (2).

The Hot Achiever (3)

The Hot Achiever is driven to excel, to win, to get ahead in order to connect with others. He lets no obstacle stand in his way. Being heart based and thus people-oriented, he cheerfully inspires others to work with him. Rather than running right over an obstacle as would a Hot Leader, the Achiever does an efficient 'end' run, thereby offending as few as possible. Because he operates at the not-quite-red-hot temperature of efficiency and smoothness, he is always under control and well presented. However, don't be fooled by his seemingly cool demeanor: he will always bring whatever heat he needs to win.

The Hot Achiever (3)	Higher Functioning	Lower Functioning
In General	• Represents the 'can-do' spirit that leads a team to the championship every time	• Shape-shifting workaholics who will do anything to impress and have 'no shame' about how they get ahead
In Meetings	• Systematically deals with barriers to change • Makes a case for change • Brings energy and teamwork to the table	• Rides roughshod over individuals • Relies on 'selling' rather than credibility

Stereotypes: Olympic Champion, Wall Street Trader, Used Car Salesman.
Examples: Mitt Romney, Bill Clinton, Harry Potter, Tom Cruise

The Cool Connector (4)

Driven to connect his inner emotions and experiences with the outer world's agenda, the Cool Connector will focus on the most heart-felt organizational values and mission rather than the needs of others. This person is highly creative, and off hours, he may express his talents in one of the arts. When an outer goal aligns with his very personal view of a situation, the Cool Connector devises solutions that draw from the strengths of his colleagues while creating a breathtakingly beautiful and unique answer to the group's challenges. The Cool Connector is one of the two most withdrawn types of leaders (along with the Cool Thinker), and his heat is more obviously apparent in his provocative creations, innovations and documents, rather than in interpersonal interactions. Typically preferring to play the #2 strategic role behind CEO, Connectors can nevertheless become quite outspoken once they give their heart to a project.

The Cool Connector (4)	Higher Functioning	Lower Functioning
In General	• Provides others with creative solutions that are unique in the marketplace of goods and ideas	• Unproductively sensitive and melancholy • Self-absorbed when unable to find anything personally meaningful (heartfelt) in the task or agenda at hand
In Meetings	• Stimulates creativity and heartfelt openness to change • Adept at highlighting the purpose of the meeting, the work, and the organization • Can provide a strategically contrarian view	• Distracted by his own emotional response to change or to the change agent himself • Creates unnecessary obstacles

Stereotype: the Artist
Examples: Jackie Onassis, Princess Diana, Bob Dylan (This type can exert very strong leadership in a room, but prefer not to take formal leadership positions.)

The Cool and Hot Provider (2)

The Cool and Hot Provider is driven to connect with others by being of service to them. In preparation for meetings, he will create meticulous and extensive written agendas and support materials, choose impeccable meeting facilities and food, and assemble the perfect cast of consultants, advisors and resource people to support the team. The Cool and Hot Provider can be gutsy and driven to help others, whether those others are shareholders or the struggling family down the street. Yet the Cool and Hot Provider feels much less compelled to act on his own behalf. Thus, he can run hot or cold, depending on for whom and for what he is fighting. There seem to be fewer leaders of this type on the world stage. Instead, the Cool and Hot Provider prefers to lead behind the scenes as a top advisor.

The Cool & Hot Provider (2)	Higher Functioning	Lower Functioning
In General	• Shepherds and rallies entire organizations to fight the world's most pressing causes against the greatest odds	• Leads indirectly through manipulation, political in-fighting, and shameless yet barely conscious self-promotion
In Meetings	• Makes participation possible for all • Brings out the best in individuals • Provides "glue" for group cohesion	• Focuses on process over task and individual needs over organizational needs

Examples: Mother Theresa, Oprah, Bill Cosby, Rahm Emmanual

THE NINE LEADERSHIP ENERGIES: THE HEAD-BASED LEADERS

Head based leaders focus intently on the world of ideas. The Hot Innovator generates endless possibilities (7), the Cool Thinker offers dispassionate wisdom (5), and the Hot and Cool Implementer provides task-oriented implementation based on previous successes (6).

The Hot Innovator (7)

The Hot Innovator is a visionary who stimulates others' imaginations with innovative responses to every hot opportunity he encounters in the organization or marketplace. Always thinking about what could go right, the Hot Innovator believes the best way to know the future is to generate endless ideas until something takes. His excitement about life's possibilities is contagious. The Hot Innovator's heat is generated by the brilliance of a wondrous idea. Being a glutton for stimulation and new information, the Hot Innovator actually enjoys opportunities to improvise solutions and explore new ways of doing things; no matter how many tries it takes for him to "get it right."

The Hot Innovator (7)	Higher Functioning	Lower Functioning
In General	• Visionary who opens our eyes to a world of ideas beyond our wildest dreams • Keeper of faith in the future	• Intellectual dilettante • Poor on follow-through • Focused neither on lasting commitment to anyone or anything but rather on what's most fun and interesting
In Meetings	• Stimulates energy and excitement and even fun into exploring the possibilities, with few preconceived notions	• Stifles participation by steering the group based on personal interests • Prefers breadth to depth and change rather than refining or editing

Examples: Steve Jobs ("Innovation distinguishes between a leader and a follower."), Sir Richard Branson, Malcolm Forbes, FDR, JFK, Newt Gingrich, Joe Biden, Ben Franklin

The Cool Thinker (5)

The Cool Thinker leads from the world of ideas, and prefers to watch and think before acting. An exquisite observer, he will station himself (metaphorically if not literally) back from the team table in order to disengage from the fray and focus on the facts. The Cool Thinker is most comfortable leading from expertise and becoming involved when and only when he has mastered the facts. He actively avoids the heat of emotional involvement, leading instead through the power of cool wisdom. However, when faced with irrationality or inefficiency, the Cool Thinker easily loses his patience, and his dispassionate words suddenly become heatedly blunt and cutting. Because he finds that interactions with others deplete his energy, the Cool Thinker often leads with few words and even less face-to-face time.

The Cool Thinker (5)	Higher Functioning	Lower Functioning
In General	• Inspires others by providing exquisite solutions to intractable problems	•Untouchable techno geek, who prefers his inner tinker-toys and computers to the outer world of action and people
In Meetings	• Attends to data and effectively articulates observations that welcome change • Systematically plans	•Becomes distracted by data at the expense of humans involved • Pays more attention to what's written than what's said

Examples: Albert Einstein, Bill Gates, Warren Buffett, Amelia Earhart, Charles Darwin

The Cool and Hot Implementer (6)

The Cool and Hot Implementer believes that when he provides and leads from an established framework, he generates a simplicity that benefits everyone. A true believer in tradition, he usually bases his framework on what he believes has worked well in the past. Whatever approach he takes, he will stay loyal to that approach to the end. This leader has a clear understanding of emergency procedures. By always picturing and preparing for the worst, the Cool and Hot Implementer insures his reliability during a crisis. He will keep the shop open and running while others are out experimenting or slacking, and he will keep everyone safe by knowing how to respond in an emergency. He is ambivalent about power, and he will sometimes reject help, even when he could use that help. This is because the Cool and Hot Implementer does not always trust people in power, even though he respects the position of power. He is more likely to play the part of loyal skeptic than of rebel. At times, his mistrusting nature leads him to fear the future; on his better days, the Cool and Hot Implementer will feel he can conquer any threats from the future. This leader can burn cool or hot, depending on his emotional state. Frequently found in a government or military position, the Cool and Hot Implementer is a 'salt of the earth' individual who does whatever is necessary to keep society ticking.

HOT LEADERS COOL FACILITATORS

The Cool and Hot Implementer (6)	Higher Functioning	Lower Functioning
In General:	• The quintessential first responder who steps forward in a crisis to quickly assess where the potential for danger lies and lead the group to safety • Loyal to others	• Paralyzed by fears and a relentless pessimism that drags the group to a halt • Relentlessly and impulsively takes risks sticking his chin into danger to prove he is unafraid
In Meetings:	• Stimulates thinking about what can go right/wrong • Pushes group persistently towards solving problems and closing the deal	• Becomes bogged down in implementation details and issues of whether something is fair or safe • Overly controlling of process and threatened by the unforeseen

Examples: Andrew Grove (Intel), Ted Turner, Richard Nixon, Harry S. Truman

LEADERSHIP TYPES BY TEMPERATURE AND ENERGY CENTER

	HOT	Cool and Hot (Cool until Not)	COOL
GUT (Drive and Power)	Hot Leaders (8) Seek safety by gaining control, pushing and provoking to get at the raw truth	Perfecters (1) Seek to either follow rules or change rules that are unjust	Cool Facilitators (9) Seek to create peace & harmony
HEART (Connection and Commitment)	Hot Achievers (3) Seek connection with others through competing and winning	Providers (2) Seek connection by being of service	Cool Connectors (4) Seek connection with others by determining what is most important and meaningful
HEAD (Thinking and Anxiety)	Hot Innovators (7) Seek what is interesting and new as an alternative to anxiety	Implementers (6) Seek predictability and something or someone worthy of their loyalty as a solution for anxiety	Cool Thinkers (5) Focus on observations and problem-solving as a way to ignore anxiety

Chapter 14
Persona Non Grata, aka
The Shadow

The cave you fear to enter holds the treasure you seek.
— Joseph Campbell

This thing of darkness I acknowledge mine. There is nothing more confining than the prison we don't know we are in.
— William Shakespeare

I looked and looked and this I came to see — that what I thought was you and you was really me and me.
— Unknown

Within every person exists more than one self: the 'persona' and the 'shadow self.' The persona is the self that one projects out into the world; it is who one chooses to be, and how one chooses to be known by his peers. The persona is defined by one's core beliefs about life and about himself. In the last chapter, you began to explore your persona, or upfront leadership type. In the first half of life, that persona dominates. Yet with continuing maturity comes the opportunity to discover and develop the shadow self. This is step two in the journey to great leadership.

Not everyone embraces or recognizes his shadow self. Within the shadows of the persona, hide the facets of personality that one may prefer not to acknowledge. Actions coming from the shadow side often meet with surprise and denial, "That's not me!" Yet the shadow self is not necessarily bad; within the shadows of the persona one may find abilities (gut), emotions (heart), or ideas and dreams (head) that are, in fact, laudable and admirable. Positive shadows typically remain undeveloped or under-developed, either because the person is unaware of their existence or because he finds those traits to be unacceptable, uncomfortably difficult or unimportant. While step two in the journey to great leadership is often initiated by a mid-life crisis, or by career derailment, it doesn't have to be. A proactive individual can begin to explore his shadow self without awaiting the drama of crisis. For example, books like *Drawing from the Right Side of the Brain* by Betty Edwards offer a reader the chance to develop shadow capabilities that he either didn't previously recognize or didn't previously value.

Jung described the conscious self (persona) and the shadow, loosely translated, as the feminine and the masculine. Accepting the shadow means accepting qualities typically associated with the opposite gender. The shadow is where one stores the unwanted parts, and this part of the self is normally visible only under the bright light of self-awareness. If one's persona is hard edged, the shadow is typically soft, approachable and even passive. If the persona is facilitative and accepting, the shadow can be judgmental and even bigoted. It is the poet that lies within the calloused leader, the enraged militant that lives within the pacifist, the lover of antiquities lying within the avant-garde musician. It is the Cool Facilitator lying in the shadow of the Hot Leader and the Hot Leader dormant in the shadow of the Cool Facilitator. The essential point is that those qualities are there all along, but hidden, ignored or forgotten.

The Shadow Knows: The Leader's Unwelcome Best Friend

Remember principle five: a great leader does not fear his shadow. In fact, the shadow is an ally in leadership. Accepting and developing the shadow traits allows a leader to recognize subtleties in temperature and choose the best response rather than the automatic response. One limits his leadership options when he excludes the leadership traits that exist in his shadow. The shadow provides a counterpoint within the self, allowing the motivational creative tension to be more effective. Without awareness and then, acceptance of the shadow, a person can't most effectively lead or facilitate. As he moves up the career ladder and his work becomes increasingly complex, only the leader who can access his shadow will have the bandwidth to use temperature strategically in his interactions and set the room temperature most effectively.

Recall principle two: once a leader has convened a meeting, his leadership will never be the same again. As a facilitator and trusted advisor to leaders, I experience this phenomenon regularly. Yet before I entered this line of work, one impromptu meeting gave me the opportunity to face my shadow side and develop my leadership capabilities.

The Shadow Emerges

"Bart, you need to come to the front desk. You're not going to believe this one".

I walked from my office in the back of the store to see what the ruckus was about. I was the 25-year-old manager of a popular outdoor store, developing my leadership skills as I applied to graduate schools. When I reached the front desk, I saw Clark Dufresne, a regular customer, standing between two of my hefty salesmen. Clark's buying sprees typically occurred on a Friday night or Saturday, when he would spend several hours looking at the latest climbing gear, mountaineering boots, and skis, and then make purchases at a scale that required a professional or executive level of disposable income. Other than being an intelligent guy who looked and acted like he had some authority, there was little remarkable about him. His strongly held and frequently voiced opinions about equipment were not unusual for the many business grad students, engineers and professionals who frequented the store.

"What's up?" I asked.

"Mr. Dufresne left the store with some items in his possession, but did not stop to pay for them. The merchandise alarms at the door sounded off and when we asked him to stop, he bolted. We finally cornered him in the other side of the parking lot," explained Jake, one of my sales clerks.

I invited the customer to come to my office along with Jake. I asked, "So what's this about, Jake?"

Clark jumped in. "Look, It's all very simple. I can clear all this up if..."

"Hold on please. I need to hear Jake's description first."

"He bolted like a jack rabbit once the alarm sounded and the chase was on for several minutes. Here's what we found." Jake pulled out a pair of mitten snow covers that retailed for around $15. Fifteen dollars? Things were not adding up at all here. I closed the door behind Jake as he left the office, and before I had returned to my desk, Clark spouted, "I've got lot's of things coming up in the next month. I'm getting married in two weeks, and in three weeks I leave the D.A.'s office to join a private practice. I'll give you a call later in the month and we can clear this up. "

He arose as if to leave. "This is just a misunderstanding," he added hastily.

"And the nature of this misunderstanding is...?"

"It was an accident...Look, here's my card. "

His card read, 'Clark Dufresne, J.D. Assistant District Attorney. I had a funny feeling I should be careful about getting any parking tickets from this point forward. "Let's just settle up and get going," Clark added.

I began to sense I was with an unrestrained Hot Leader who was jumping to conclusions about what temperature would help his cause.

"Clark, give me a few minutes." He went to sit outside my door again, looking as if he had simply come to inquire about a special order on some climbing boots.

Just then, another member of the management team walked in. I reviewed the situation with him. What consequence could we devise that would not blow up this guy's life over a pair of mitten covers? Contributions to charity? Community service? An apology? I then recalled a previous Saturday at the store, when I had the police arrest two teenagers for shoplifting. Suddenly, my direction was clear. I asked Clark to return and take a seat in my office. I picked up the receiver from it's cradle (this was the old days), but Clark laid his hand across the cradle to break the connection.

I looked him squarely in the eyes. "Get back in your seat or I will suggest to the cop who is about to walk through that door that you attempted to physically intimidate me as well as shoplift."

Clark sat, while I finished the call to the police station. The patrol officer arrived quickly.

Clark, true to his automatic response, blurted, "Look, Officer, I'll explain."

The officer looked at me inquisitively.

"He stole these items from the store," I explained.

The officer ordered Clark to stand spread-eagle across my desk, and proceeded to frisk him for weapons.

This hyper-successful 30-year-old was on the brink of personal and professional breakthroughs, until he shoplifted a minor item from his favorite store and resisted arrest. How is his story relevant to our discussion of the shadow self's effect on leadership?

Here's the analysis from the leadership perspective: Clark was a Hot Leader, accustomed to moving quickly, calling the shots, speaking boldly and getting what he wanted. His persona was the leader in control, top dog. Many of these qualities are well suited to the D.A. role, both in the courtroom and in leading a prosecutor's team. In fact, these qualities probably led to his rapid career success. Yet two other very important qualities lay dormant in the shadow of this Hot Leader: a trusting nature, and a risk taker.

Clark was about to trust a new wife, trust a new set of professional partners, and maybe trust himself in new ways. Yet he remained blissfully unaware (or totally in denial) that the prospect of entering this next phase of life was scaring the hell out of him. Clark could have avoided this bizarre meltdown in my store if he had simply faced the truth: I am about to do something that doesn't feel like me, trusting others with my entire future. I'm not into delegating control, but I need to delegate some control if I am going to 'lead' my life into the future. I've got to face that trusting and taking the risk of releasing the reins is what I'm about to do and it scares the hell out of me.

In terms of temperature, Clark reflexively dealt with everything by heating it up. He managed to light a fuse under my staff, under me, and under the police officer by incessantly pushing for control. Had he advocated for himself at a lower temperature, he could have slowed the process and increased the chances that I would go easy on him. Instead, his gut-laden words suggested strongly to everyone that he was not interested in an effective interaction. He was interested only in having his own way. That may be action, but it is not leadership. Every interaction is both a test and demonstration of leadership.

At this point in Clark's life, he needed to cool things to gain an objective perspective and understanding. Most of all, Clark needed to get to a temperature where he could deal with the yearnings of his heart towards others (and others' towards him). He did none of those things, so his shadow jumped out and bit him hard.

My automatic response would have been to chill the situation and give Clark an out. However, the ten-minute conversation with a member of my management staff helped to stop my reflexive response. It gave me a moment to have an internal conversation with my own shadow during this leadership challenge: It's true that I don't like being harsh, punitive or dogmatic. But this situation calls for clear, definitive action, regardless of the pain it causes someone else. In fact, if I don't face my own reflexive avoidance of causing Clark pain, he'll just go do something else to cause more pain to himself and others. I realized my job was to let the truth reveal itself by standing my ground without heating the situation further, and provoking my staff to act unprofessionally. My awareness of my own shadow, of what I liked to avoid, allowed me to view the full menu of leadership options, not just the 'chef's specials' or 'kid's menu'.

The rundown? When a Hot Leader (Clark) faces a Cool Facilitator (Me), the Cool Facilitator wants to turn the heat off by minimizing the seriousness of the situation, until the Cool Facilitator takes a step back to clear his head. He then realizes he must access his own shadow Hot Leader in order to bring the situation to an appropriate resolution.

Typically, we'd rather stick with our familiar interaction temperature and let someone else mess with those things in our shadows which make us irritable, uncomfortable or confused. This avoids the truth that a variety of temperatures are required in every leadership position, and in every type of interaction.

When a Cool Facilitator is in collaboration with his shadow, he has the guts to take bold action, saying only what is absolutely necessary and driving towards the goal. Imagine a Cool Facilitator zooming in hard:

"Do you want me here or not? I get paid either way."

"I don't see the point of this conversation. It's one big cop-out."

"I need to know how you wish to proceed with this meeting. My job is to run the meeting and your job is to make decisions and get moving. I'm doing my job. When are you going to do yours?"

Similarly, when a Hot Leader is in collaboration with his shadow, he'll pause to tell a story with heart that explains his position, crack a joke at his own expense, or express an emotion other than anger in a serious manner. Imagine a Hot Leader stepping back and admitting:

"I'm embarrassed to say that I don't really know what is going on here. Could someone help me out?"

"I just came down hard on all of you about this issue. I would appreciate your honest reactions to what I said and how I said it."

"I suck at running meetings, but I'm concerned at how we are falling behind our deadlines. We need suggestions about what to do next."

Unacknowledged Shadows Are Serious Business

The story of Sol and Frank, two Heat-Seeking Leaders working in the US aviation industry, provides a dramatic example of how a leader can make a positive difference by collaborating with his shadow side, and how a leader ignoring his shadow side can contribute to a tragic outcome.

In the earlier days of the US space program, two particular types of leaders populated the US aviation industry: Hot Leaders and Hot Innovators. The Hot Leaders were, for the most part, veterans of WWII and former test and fighter pilots, the Chuck Yeager's of the era. Their gut-driven intensity and love of 'testing' their strength against others made them successful pilots and contributed to their rapid rise to the top executive ranks of the aerospace companies.

Frank, the president of the rocketry division of a major defense contractor, was one such leader. He was known for his swashbuckling arrogance and breaches of etiquette with the starred generals who were his division's customers: at the Pentagon, with the Royal Air Force in England, and at NASA. Frank habitually greeted the generals by their first names, and was the only vendor who dared behave so inappropriately. While he got away with his irreverence for a while, eventually Frank's behavior threatened to affect business. The company's bread and butter product, upon which the enormous division had based its growth, was no longer enough to keep its vast manufacturing facilities fully engaged.

At this same time, NASA issued a request for proposals to design and manufacture the manned space module that would later become the Apollo spacecraft. Competition was fierce among the usual corporations capable of bringing such engineering and manufacturing expertise to the table. Frank appointed his V.P. of engineering and manufacturing, Sol, to head the proposal team. Sol was a Hot Innovator type, capable of making the bold, even harsh decisions at which Hot Leaders excelled. Though interested in others, Hot Innovators typically relegate compassion to their shadow, infatuated as they are with new ideas, innovations and approaches. Working in the flow with what is interesting is more pleasurable for them than the irritation of spending engineering time worrying about what's fair to the people involved.

Sol was aware that he could be abrasive in his impatience. As he had risen through the ranks of the company, he had learned to modulate the heat he reflexively brought to things. Sol prided himself on his reputation as 'tough but fair,' and he had built a division that made money all the while commanding loyalty from the many Cool Thinkers who tend to populate the executive ranks of engineering firms. Sol brought heart energy into his leadership. While the exciting hardware he and his colleagues designed could easily seduce most head energy types like him, Sol had developed the capacity to keep his focus on the humans who would operate the innovative machines. In meetings, Sol would relay a good joke, an interesting story, or find other ways to show his compassion for employees to bring the room temperature to the Engaged Field.

Once, while touring a newly designed and completed missile bunker, Sol abruptly stopped the entourage of proud Air Force brass. When they entered the control room, Sol sat in the controller's chair, and declared, "You've got to change this design." He pointed out the window. "You've given your man at the control panel a direct line of sight to the bunker itself. These missiles will never be 100% reliable. Do you want that man to be in the direct line of fire of debris when a missile aborts and self-destructs?"

By communicating with the combined wisdom of all three energy centers, Sol engendered the respect of his peers. The Air Force engineers promptly re-configured the bunker, and all of the others, at no little expense. Sol was operating not only from his comfort zone, as an innovator and a problem-solving engineer, but also from an area typically delegated to the shadows of his personality type: genuine concern for and loyalty to others. In this instance, Sol's ability to utilize his shadow-self may have actually saved lives.

When the Apollo competition was announced, Sol used his hot leadership style to approach his boss, Frank, about their plans. Knowing that a pure oxygen cabin atmosphere could ignite in the presence of an unintended source of heat, such as an errant spark, Sol warned, "Frank, word on the street is that the bid most likely to be competitive with ours is going to spec for a pure oxygen atmosphere for the astronauts. That's insanity and you know it, so I know you will be happy that we are going with a mixed oxygen environment."

Frank was happy to have something to crow about. Unfortunately, his unrestrained arrogance didn't help him sell his product. The competitors' design was in the lead at NASA. Sol believed the reason that his proposal was quickly losing ground was that some of NASA's military advisors could not bear Frank's aggressiveness, not to mention his breaches of military etiquette.

Seeing that Frank's failure to trust the heart wisdom within his shadow could result in deadly consequences, Sol suggested Frank take a more heartfelt approach in selling the design. Seeking harmony and connection could have helped Frank achieve his goals. Instead, Frank's gut-based drive for action repeatedly provoked the NASA leaders, who were estranged from the perspective-seeking head energy in their own shadows. They themselves remained stuck in their stubborn Hot Leadership and refused to consider the designs that Frank, "that disrespectful s.o.b.," had to offer.

It appeared to Sol that the Apollo competition had become a battle of personas, rather than an honest assessment of the best possible approach to the engineering and safety challenges. Had the decision makers at NASA been willing or able to operate from their cooler, more thoughtful shadow sides, they might have been able to say, "Frank is an s.o.b., but rather than getting provoked into losing perspective, let's focus on finding the best solution for our astronauts."

Sol grew desperate, as Frank continued to ignore his advice. Determined to 'blow the whistle' he broke protocol and directly approached several members of the corporate board about his boss' indirect and unconscious sabotage of the company's bid, to no avail.

Frank continued to lead the interaction with NASA and, in the end, the project was awarded to another company. On January 17th, 1967, three Apollo astronauts died on the launch pad as a result of a fire in the Apollo module's pure oxygen cabin atmosphere. Sol was grief-stricken, along with the nation.

Unfortunately, strategic leadership of temperature did not result in success, in this case. Yet without it, the case would have been closed and Sol's truth never would have been heard. As he related this story to me year's later, Sol was still deeply regretful. In his view, the meetings leading up to the Apollo's launch could have led to a positive outcome if the players involved had been willing to open themselves to the truth about their leadership styles. When leaders in any organization refuse to work with both their persona and their shadow selves, the truth becomes the victim. They become unable to lead meetings into the Engaged Field that promotes the truths essential for success.

So, how does a leader learn to work with his persona and shadow sides? By becoming uncomfortable…

CHAPTER 15
DISCOMFORT AND YOUR SHADOW: YOUR RELIABLE TEMPERATURE COACH

Here's the truth about leadership: discomfort is one's closest coach, always at hand, always giving instant feedback. Those activities that irritate, annoy, or cause discomfort, and those qualities or emotions that one wishes to diminish often hold the greatest upside potential for one's leadership. Why? Discomfort leads an individual to discover his shadow.

Being a seeker of the truth has never been a job for the faint of heart. Yet the average person makes it infinitely more difficult than it has to be by ignoring information that is already at his disposal.

How can you tell when the shadow, the internal emotional coach, is trying to whip you into shape? If you find yourself thinking, or saying, "It all makes me uncomfortable," or, "It just plain ticks me off," then stop what you're doing and listen to the rest of what your mind is saying to you.

Tracking 'negative' emotions, feelings and experiences, rather than simply putting them aside, opens the door to the knowledge of the shadow one needs to become a great leader. These sensations are the flags, or the 'police tape' that alert someone when they've stepped over a line, from comfort to discomfort, from what he knows to what he doesn't, from what he likes, to what he would like to avoid.

Developing your leadership competencies involves using temperature to invite the painful truth into interaction. Hot Leaders often ignore their own pain and the pain of others, and distract themselves with fast action or 'hot' pleasures. Cool Facilitators often ignore pain, through efforts to remain cool, calm and collected, such as running, cycling, hiking, gardening, meditation, music, or anything that will help them forget the frustrations and discomforts caused by heat and emotional or physical pain.

Like great leaders, great athletes approach pain differently. Contrary to popular wisdom, elite athletes do not simply ignore pain. Instead, they treat pain as essential data, a given part of training and performing. Though nothing to be sought or savored (we save the term 'masochism' for those who revel in pain), pain can be an indicator of progress, an important element of one's personal dashboard by which one fine-tunes his training methods and schedule. Great athletes do not slavishly respond to every unwelcome muscle twitch but meticulously accept every twitch as useful data to be analyzed in the light of all the information available about the body. They use the data to learn which training, competitive schedule and strategy, and which events are most effective for them.

How does the pain of irritation, discomfort or boredom help one become more effective at leading meetings? When a leader understands more about his upfront leadership types and his shadows, he can increase his dexterity with temperature management. Meetings (and thus leadership) suffer when one does not recognize and work through his discomfort, disdain, and/or disinterest in his shadow.

A shortcut is to recognize that each upfront type has a set of shadows. As viewed on a chart, these shadow twins appear to be the 'wings' on either side of the upfront type. For example, it is common for Type 8 Hot Leaders to find descriptions of their shadow somewhere in Type 7 or Type 9.

The persona's shadow twins are analogous to the complementary relationship of the body's muscle 'twins'. Ever had low back or neck pain? Shin splints? Knee pain? There are many causes for each of these symptoms, but a very common cause is an imbalance between what are normally complementary sets of muscles. Most muscles (agonists that cause the movement to occur) have their counterpart (antagonists) which pull in the opposite direction. The biceps and the triceps are counterpart muscles. There are also synergists and fixators, which help steady the body while the agonist and antagonist are doing their work. One's entire ability to balance is the result of a second-by-second creative tension between entire sets of muscles from the feet up through the neck. Those complementary muscles are essential to the body's ability to function, but like the neglected shadow selves, the neglected complementary muscles reveal themselves in unpleasant ways. When one overdevelops a set of muscles, such as the calves by jogging, one invites trouble from the shadow muscles around the shins.

Wings: A Likely Place to look for Your Shadow

Each leadership type has two wings. They are the leadership types adjacent to either side of our primary leadership type. People usually find one wing that they easily recognize as part of themselves. It is in the other wing that you can often find your shadow

HOW TO USE THE WING CHART

STEP 1: Choose an upfront leadership type from the middle column, and let yourself feel your physical, emotional and intellectual reaction to the beliefs to either side. If you don't feel at least a twinge from anything you read in this table, you either have not chosen an upfront type that really describes you, or you are asleep at the wheel.

STEP 2: Envision acting from the shadow sides of your persona type.

STEP 3: Envision how someone else with each of these beliefs would respond to various challenging situations.

The more comfortable you feel imagining such scenarios, the greater the breadth of your leadership. Developing a sense of ease with your shadow will increase your ability to creatively react to and mange the temperatures you encounter. Otherwise, your leadership will suffer and others will notice you reacting automatically, rather than strategically, to temperature.

An example would be a Hot Innovator (7) like Steve Jobs. He is able to move beyond the heat of exciting new ideas to value the cooler

THE WING CHART

WING Beliefs	UPFRONT LEADERSHIP Beliefs	WING Beliefs
(9)Trust the process, bend and go with the flow. Harmony beats conflict anytime.	(1) Play by the rules and, if necessary, take a stand on principle. Things can be better, even perfected. Principles come before individual persons.	(2) People's individual needs come before rules and principles. My needs will be met if I provide for your needs first.
(1) Play by the rules and, if necessary, take a stand on principle. Things can be better, even perfected. Principles come before individual persons	(2) People's individual needs come before rules and principles. My needs will be met if I provide for your needs first.	(3) Just do it. What do emotions, needs or principles have to do with winning or even finishing?
(2) People's individual needs come before rules and principles. My needs will be met if I provide for your needs first.	(3) Just do it. What do emotions, needs or principles have to do with winning or even finishing?	(4) If you'd just consult your emotions then you'd know what is really meaningful.
(3) Just do it. What do emotions, needs or principles have to do with winning or even finishing?	(4) If you'd just consult your emotions then you'd know what is really meaningful.	(5) I act only after I objectively assess and master the data. So leave me alone.

temperatures that engender loyalty and commitment to his team. He values the systems that successful implementation requires (Type 6), and values making the tough choices that brings an idea into production (Type 8) before moving on to the next exciting thing (Type 7). The combination of the three leadership beliefs and their range of temperatures produce a powerfully effective leader.

The Leadership Journey:
The Three Stages of Allying with Your Shadow

Learning to include your shadow allows you to grow from in-authentic (unaware) to self-aware, and finally to a fully engaged leader. Once you determine the leadership and shadow types, you will be able to manage temperatures in a more strategic and less reflexive manner. The

THE WING CHART

(4) If you'd just consult your emotions then you'd know what is really meaningful.	(5) I act only after I objectively assess and master the data. So leave me alone.	(6) Reliability, Safety, Loyalty and commitment: Why mess with what works?
(5) I act only after I objectively assess and master the data. So leave me alone.	(6) Reliability, safety, loyalty and commitment: Why mess with what works?	(7) Let's check out something new and exciting. Faith in the future is the way.
(6) Reliability, safety, loyalty and commitment: Why mess with what works?	(7) Let's check out something new and exciting. Faith in the future is the way.	(8) No one is going to mess with me or mine. I decide the future.
(7) Let's check out something new and exciting. Faith in the future is the way.	(8) No one is going to mess with me or mine. I decide the future.	(9)Trust the process, bend and go with the flow. Harmony beats conflict anytime.
(8) No one is going to mess with me or mine. I decide the future.	(9)Trust the process, bend and go with the flow. Harmony beats conflict anytime.	(1) Play by the rules and, if necessary, take a stand on principle: things can be better, even perfected. Principles come before individual persons

goal is not to become another type; the goal is to accept the inherent value of the other types within you.

Getting to this stage of understanding is a process rather than an event. It takes time. Great leaders place importance on making the journey but also cut themselves some slack when they fall short of the ideal of being a fully engaged and authentic leader at every moment.

They know there are three stages to this journey of awareness:

Stage One: The inauthentic leader believes in the limitations of his persona, and is unaware of other facets of his personality. "I am these things," he says to himself. "I am not those other things. They are of little importance to my work."

Stage Two: Through self-exploration, the self-aware leader has learned about himself and his capabilities, but has not accepted the non-dominant traits in his shadow. "I am these things," he says. "I know about and can do those other things, but I prefer not to. Anyway, I'm not particularly adept at them and they are unimportant."

Stage Three: Through hard work, honest exploration and open-mindedness, the engaged leader knows who he is and accepts all facets of his being. "I am all of these things and I do all these things, guided by my head, heart and gut," he says. "I work to become capable at what was previously in my shadow."

Label Your Reactions to Increase Your Awareness of Your Shadow

If you pay attention, you will notice specific indicators that you are venturing into uncomfortable territory. The tightness in the neck, sinking feeling in the gut, and distractibility that you are so adept at ignoring are potential allies. While you focus on the Power Point presentation in front of you, your body, mind and heart are trying to tell you something equally (if not more) important. To tend to your physical discomforts may momentarily slow your pursuit of the day's goals, but will speed your pursuit of self-awareness.

Ask yourself this essential question:

Do I know what causes this discomfort?

Next, ask yourself the FIVE WHY'S to get to the true message your gut, head and heart are sending you.

For example, if you notice increasing tension in your neck, ask yourself:

1. *WHY* is this happening?
   Answer One: It's been a long day.

2. *WHY?*
   Answer Two: I find it a strain to concentrate on these slides.

3. *WHY?*
   Answer Three: Because I have more interesting things to do that I'd prefer to deal with instead.

4. *WHY?*

Answer Four: I didn't get around to delegating the task to my V.P. of Operations.

5. *WHY?*

Answer Five: Because I tend to avoid putting my foot down and taking control with my staff.

Bingo! You have bumped into the fact that your avoidance of taking control is a pain in the neck for you. Is there something about heat that you tend to avoid? Do you need to stretch yourself to become more comfortable with heat when it is needed? Does your staff operate at a higher temperature than you, and make you want to flee?

Checklist of Commonly Dismissed Signs

Everyone experiences inner tension at times, even tough leaders and serene facilitators. Any leader who does not have moments of discomfort, displeasure and stress is not really leading. Can you identify your personal red flags that signal you are in distress? Do you recognize the subtle cautionary yellow flags that precede a bump on the road?

Consider the answers to the following questions to see how you experience inner tension:

☐ How much must you lower your rearview mirror when re-entering your car at day's end to compensate for the muscle contraction of the day?

☐ How often do you find yourself fidgeting in your seat, jiggling your legs under the table or pacing?

☐ Take a deep breath and let your shoulders and arms hang in response to gravity. How many additional inches now separate your shoulders from your ears?

☐ How often do you find yourself holding your breath or forcing your breath through clenched teeth?

☐ How often does your g.i. tract produce audible grumblings and gurglings?

☐ Are your hands clenched or at rest?

☐ Are your arms folded or relaxed?

☐ Do you have sweaty palms, forehead, underarms or feet?

☐ Do you smack or bite your lips, squint or otherwise contort the muscles in your face?

☐ How often is your daydreaming unrelated to the task? Are you easily distracted? Do you return to a room to find something and forget why you entered?

☐ Do you ever stand in the shower and forget whether you have shampooed your hair?

Here are some other physical signs that you may be experiencing inner tension:

☐ Blushing.

☐ Sudden changes in physical or intellectual energy.

☐ Increase in error rate and/or forgetting.

☐ Increased difficulty forgiving others.

☐ Increase in needless worrying.

☐ Increased compulsivity in both positive (exercising, competitive sports, organizing neatness) and negative activities (recreational substances, eating, gambling, risk-taking)

☐ Speaking too rapidly or slowly, at increasingly louder or softer tones. Repeating yourself.

☐ Experiencing sudden, unexpected fears and phobias.

Observation suggests that each upfront leadership type tends to experience certain discomfort signs more than others.

Leadership Type	Common Somatic/Behavioral Flags of Discomfort
The Hot and Cool Perfecter (1)	Anger, neck/back tightness/pain, impatience, disdain, hyper-criticality
The Hot and Cool Provider (2)	Overeating, anger, aggression
The Hot Achiever (3)	Hyperactivity/workaholism/ Pressured (quickened) speech
The Cool Connector (4)	Avoidance, fluctuations in energy, Feeling disdain towards others
The Cool Thinker (5)	Boredom, withdrawal, hyperactivity
The Hot and Cool Implementer (6)	Anxiety,impatience, obsessiveness (organizing etc.), g.i. tract issues
The Hot Innovator (7)	Boredom, restlessness, distractibility/ day-dreaming
The Hot Leader (8)	Withdrawal (I'm taking my ball and going home), Increased impulsivity/ anger/heat
The Cool Facilitator (9)	Neck/back tension, worry and anxiety, over-talking a point

Becoming guilty or anxious about the presence of these signs will not help you develop your leadership skills. As the professional athlete uses physical pain as feedback to help him improve his performance, so accepting these signs as useful data will help you to calibrate your leadership behaviors for the most successful outcomes. Discomfort can be your closest ally in the journey to great leadership, because the more you understand yourself, the more effective you can be in supporting others.

CHAPTER 16
PARTNERSHIPS BETWEEN LEADERS OF DIFFERENT TYPES

Why not simply choose a partner or 'hire' someone with the same type as your shadow to backfill for your own weaknesses and blind spots? This is certainly a viable alternative, but not without risk. Let's pause briefly to look at one highly successful leader who did just that: Franklin Roosevelt.

FDR was a Hot Innovator, the eternal optimist in spite of a bout with adult-onset polio that left him physically crippled. Buoyant, fascinating, at times arrogant, FDR was entranced with the art of conversation and with the grand characters of the era. Compassion, loyalty and a true interest in others were relegated to his shadow.

His wife Eleanor, a Hot and Cool Provider, supplied the necessary elements missing from FDR's persona: the common touch, the true concern for and commitment to others. FDR valued his wife's awareness of others and recognized it as an essential ability that he neither had nor wished to have. Eleanor was not the least hesitant about heating up conversations about these things. Her complimentary leadership gave FDR's presidency lasting traction and public support. Yet she could not provide her husband with the awareness that would have been present had he taken on these challenges himself.

Avoiding his shadow had negative consequences for his presidency. His heated attempt to 'pack' the Supreme Court, conceived in isolation but for one close advisor, was received with hostility and reflected Roosevelt's lack of awareness of the political temperature. His poor assessment of the nation's mood left his supporters aghast and his opponents hysterical in their contempt. It seems the President was also unaware of the power of manipulating temperature. This was reflected in his relationship, or lack of one, with Vice President Harry Truman. Roosevelt selected Truman because of the good will that was engendered by the latter's work leading the cost-cutting Truman Committee. Yet Roosevelt had never met with his future partner privately, until the moment he invited Truman to join him on his ticket. Consciously or unconsciously, FDR picked Truman, a specific shadow twin (a Hot and Cool Implementer) knowing he would remain loyal and committed to supporting FDR's policies. Exhibiting the loyalty so characteristic of the type, Truman never turned on FDR although FDR completely neglected him during the remainder of their work together. Ultimately, Truman was able to assume the Presidency in spite of the complete lack of preparation provided by FDR. (Forget about bad leadership in bad meetings; this was a case of no leadership in no meetings!) This failure to prepare was all the more notable given the obvious fact that his coronary heart disease was rendering FDR's ability to complete his fourth term doubtful.

Expect The Unexpected When Hiring a Shadow Twin As a Partner

Several years ago, when an organization was preparing to transition from its charismatic founder to a long-term professional president, the Board of Directors hired me as an Interim CEO. A primary qualification for this six-month assignment was my ability to lead without ego and to bring various factions together. In other words, the Board was attracted to the idea of a Cool Facilitator as leader.

One day, the phone rang as I entered the office. When I answered, I heard, "I want her out and I want her out today!!" The rage coming out of the phone was transparent and powerful, the kind of from-the-gut anger of a Hot Leader who feels betrayed, or at least, misled.

"Let's start with, who is 'her'?" I responded, without needing to ask who was calling. It was Prasad, the board chair; his style was unmistakable.

"I mean Sarah. She misled me about her personal background, and that puts in question the integrity of all of her work here. She needs to go!"

I gave Prasad a few minutes to air his barely controlled fury and let the temperature come down a bit, but it didn't. At last, seeing that the call was not going to cool off enough for us to connect, I zeroed in to where he was and pushed back. "I can't fire her and I won't. She's my employee not yours. If you think this is a policy issue, then let me know what that is."

"She lied to me."

"And that lie was...?"

"She didn't tell me about her background."

"Did she lie about it?"

"By omission."

"Are you ready for litigation from her and from the state since it would be illegal for me to fire her on this basis?"

"It can't be. I just won't have her here."

"Well, I don't get paid enough to be involved in litigation."

The sputtering on Prasad's end was loud but unintelligible.

"I'm tied up until later in the day," I finished. " Think about it and tell me where you are with this. I'm glad to hear more." I hung up the phone.

I was surprised by the subject of the call but not by the fireworks. Prasad was a brilliant, inspirational leader who always charged the room with heat. There was no such thing as a cool meeting with him in the room. On the other hand, the chair had not seen my shadow until that moment.

In effect, I was saying to Prasad: "I dare you to let this boil over!!", which is a most un-cool facilitator-like stance. It was also a way of telling him to act from his shadow for a change and calm down. With my heated response, I let Prasad know that I wouldn't and couldn't do the calming. The overheated leader would need to try some self-soothing.

By that afternoon, Prasad had in fact cooled himself down and we were able to resolve the issue effectively.

In that situation, I could have taken the typical position of the Cool Facilitator and pulled away to cool the temperature of the conversation: "This sounds like an important issue. Why don't you explain again the entire situation so that I am certain I get it, and then blah- blah-bity- blah."

However, it would have been a waste of valuable time in that instance. I assessed that the situation was not boiling over, though it was red hot. I could see that the chair would neither let me cool him down, nor let the situation boil over, because he was not prepared to have me leave. My choice to push back inspired Prasad to retreat and to cool himself down.

Many heat-seeking leaders can be moved toward their Cool Facilitator shadows with a strong push. They learn primarily through heat, including what looks to others like arguing. At the end of the second conversation, I further moderated things, bringing them to the heart range of temperature. At this range, we were able to reconnect our usually fine relationship with a bit of humor:

"By the way, did you think you hired a wimp who will do what you say automatically?" I asked. "I know better than to think you'd do such a wuss thing."

This is an example of the twin sets (eight and nine, in my case) containing a range of qualities, that when combined, produce unusually potent forms of leadership. The qualities inherent in a leader's shadow twins give him the capability to move relationships through the range of temperatures and thus, through the individual and group discovery of core beliefs that help participants as well as the organization. Only leaders who are on good speaking terms with their shadow parts make the best use of everyone they hire.

CHAPTER 17
THE STRETCH AND ESCAPE ROUTES TO LEADERSHIP

Understanding one's leadership type and shadow twins is an important step in learning how to recognize and strategically use temperature. There are two additional concepts that every great leader should understand: the 'stretch route' and the 'escape route."

These concepts are inspired by the writing of Don Riso and Russ Hudson. They introduce 'The Direction of Growth' and 'The Direction of Stress' in *The Wisdom of the Enneagram* (Bantam Books, New York, NY, 1999).

The concept is simple: there are times when a leader behaves so uncharacteristically it can seem like he's another person. He seems to be moving beyond the boundaries of his persona and shadow twins. Yet he does not become another leadership type as much as he adds the energy and focus of that type to his existing motivations and attitudes. In doing so, the leader is taking a new path.

Sometimes the path is challenging, and the leader is operating at peak performance. I call this path the stretch route. At other times, a leader hits an obstacle that knocks him off track in his career. The event might be as minor as an important meeting going awry, or as major as losing a promotion or a experiencing a health crisis. Such derailers often send the leader running to the comfort of what I call the escape route. The escape route often feels comforting and familiar, but it does not promote a leader's growth.

Each persona has an associated stretch route and escape route, which I describe in the following tables. I have also added data points about the shadows. You can use this information to explore which persona and which shadow types apply to you.

As you examine this material, remember these three things:

1. Pondering which leadership type best describes you contains as much value as the actual decision. 'trying on,' each type will increase your awareness of yourself and others.

2. The specified stretch routes for each type, for instance, are only the most likely of a number of routes for growth that one may encounter. One may find oneself traveling down other escape routes, as well. Shadow types (wings) are also possible though less likely routes.

3. It is not unusual for the escape route to be to the lower functioning aspects of a type. Conversely, the stretch route involves traveling to the higher functioning aspects of a type.

Example of a Hot and Cool Perfecter (Type One)

A high-end retailer, Jeremy's typical leadership style was cool and hands off. He set expectations and expected others to comply. They usually did. However, when Jeremy needed to push, he simply used the stare, a characteristic look that was nearly impossible to imitate, try as some of his employees might. A single cool stare from Jeremy was many times more motivating than the hottest bark. Yet the retailer demonstrated very well how the switch from cool to hot leadership does not require volume or overt emotion. When the stare was not sufficient motivation, Jeremy usually pushed people to action by posing the question, a calmly delivered pointed query that let his employees know they were on shaky ground. Regardless of the situation, when people were not meeting his expectations, Jeremy would ask, "If you were in my shoes, what would you do?" Posing the question usually generated enough heat to get someone moving.

My meetings with him followed a consistent pattern: We exchanged pleasantries, and checked in about recent important events, then Jeremy placed a problem on the table, listened intently to my response, and peppered me with questions. Inevitably, he would think one of my answers was one sentence longer than necessary, so he would give me the stare. Our rapport was good enough that he rarely needed to subject me to the heat of the question.

Despite the general effectiveness of the stare and the question, there were some situations that called for even more heat. Like most Hot and Cool Perfecters, Jeremy could generate serious heat when acting in defense of a principle. In one such instance, Jeremy decided to take on the big guys: UPS and the Teamsters.

Jeremy felt small businesses like his were getting poorer service than the larger businesses. Larger businesses had large loading docks, or delivery sites inside large buildings, which were often far from the dock. Understandably, UPS charged a large 'inside delivery fee' for the added work of bringing a package inside, especially since it often meant the driver would spend time climbing flights of stairs or travelling in an elevator. However, UPS also charged the inside delivery fee to small businesses that had a small dock, or none at all. The distance from the exposed dock to the safety of the receiving room was a mere five feet. Jeremy didn't see why small businesses should be charged a large fee simply for a driver to walk five extra feet.

Against the advice of his friends, his colleagues, his lawyers, his family, and myself, Jeremy decided to act on his principles; he picked a fight over exactly where UPS' drivers should leave shipments on his loading dock. Choosing to lead this fight took considerable courage as the Teamsters were known for their combativeness and threatening manner.

Jeremy barked at any driver who did not place parcels inside the door of the receiving room. If the driver ignored Jeremy's barking, and still refused to comply, Jeremy would refuse the shipment. The drivers hated this, because each refused shipment entailed extra paperwork and extra physical work.

Jeremy was picking a fight against great odds and placing himself and his business at some risk, but his take was that he was fighting on behalf of all small businesses. His take was slightly clouded by emotion, however.

While Jeremy told himself and everyone else that this fight was all

THE HOT AND COOL PERFECTER (1)	Core Motivations
The Upfront Self	"It's the principle of the thing: Things can always be better. Stand up for what's right."
The Shadows' truths	(2,9) Other people's feelings and harmony come first.
The Shadows' Question	"Can you stop and be here now to take into account others' feelings and harmony?
The Upfront Self's Mistruth (about the shadows)	"Focusing on others rather than on perfection will cause me to lose control."
The Stretch (when feeling at one's best)	(7) Spontaneously exploring and enjoying exciting possibilities trumps unproductive excessive concern with perfection.
The Escape Route (Under stress)	(4) Emotions trump principles and analysis.

about principles, the truth was that this "David & Goliath" conflict sent Jeremy on a trip down his escape route to Cool Connector. The Cool Connector sometimes takes the contrarian position in order to feel like an individual. In finding the unique approach to a problem, he reassures himself that he has a special place in the world. Had Jeremy truly been operating from his dominant leadership type and defending his principles, he could have chosen to fight one of many other, more important, issues affecting his business. Had he been operating from his dominant leadership type, he probably would have achieved the desired results, in large part because he would have chosen a more logical issue to address. In this case, the heat between the business owner and the freight company continued for some time. Predictably, Jeremy made no progress with UPS.

However, Jeremy did make significant progress towards accomplishing his original goal, to have the drivers bring the parcels the five feet across the dock into the safety and shelter of the building. He did this by traveling his stretch route to the Hot Innovator (Type Seven). The Innovator's prime motivation is to find something more interesting than the preoccupations and anxieties of daily life. He is drawn to innovate because it provides an opportunity to make life interesting and fun. The experience can be as important as the end result.

Over the course of many daily five-minute interactions, a grudging admiration between Jeremy and the drivers evolved. They developed a ritual of joking and teasing each other whenever they crossed paths, which lowered the heat from boiling to merely simmering. They tried to outdo each other, inventing new ways to get under the others' skin. Jeremy might tease a driver about whose favorite baseball team had won the night before, while another driver might tell Jeremy "I'll bet you a fiver that my UPS truck with a full load could take that dinky foreign job of yours any day." Each respected the other's strength and they became comrades in the common struggle of daily work. In the end, the drivers placed the parcels just inside the receiving room door, without charging Jeremy the inside delivery fee. In this example, the Innovator allowed the temperature of the interaction to evolve, rather than remaining stuck at the unhelpful temperature it had reached.

As this course of events demonstrates, Jeremy had a knack for moving to his stretch route just in time to prevent his travels down his escape route from overheating or freezing the situation. His ability to move from his sometimes ill-considered contrarian stance saved him on many occasions, and the bold actions he took while utilizing various aspects of his leadership styles earned him notoriety among retailers in his industry. In fact, Jeremy became so well known that a columnist from an influential business paper in NYC began covering his strategies on a regular basis.

An Example of a Hot and Cool Provider (Type Two)

Gillis was an individual with considerable wealth and a complex financial situation. As such, he required more than a computer with QuickBooks™ to manage his money. It was essential that Gillis have a fully staffed family office to manage every aspect of his financial and business life. Nick, the President of that office, oversaw thirty employees and a legally very complex financial portfolio. But this story is not about Gillis, and it's not about Nick. It's about Zach.

When Gillis asked me to assemble and lead a team that would

evaluate the health of his organization, I invited Zach, a CPA and Hot and Cool Provider, to join us. I had met Zach in one of my leadership workshops, and knew he would be a valuable asset to the team. As it turns out, his presence was more beneficial than I could have imagined.

When Zach met Gillis, he felt an instant connection and was fully motivated to look out for Gillis' interests. Zach threw himself wholeheartedly into pouring through the financial information. Despite the heat of his commitment, Zach kept the process cool to be certain he caught every detail. While he crossed the t's and dotted the i's, others on the team became hot and impatient. The purpose of our project was to determine if any financial processes might be handled in a more efficient or more appropriate manner. To the hot types on our team, it seemed like Zach was handling his tasks inefficiently by moving so slowly, until Zach stumbled upon some information that suggested financial impropriety within the family office.

Zach had suspected inappropriate use of Gillis' resources from the start, but he had also hoped he was wrong. When he discovered financial expenditures with little-to-no paper trail, he presumed they led to proof of fraudulent activity. Among other things, Zach found investments in start-ups that had no evidence of approval by Gillis. Further,

THE HOT AND COOL PROVIDER	Core Motivations
The upfront self	"My needs will be met if I provide for your needs first."
The shadows' truth	(1,3) It's not all about people: There's principles and life's goals.
The shadow's question	Can you for once put yourself first?
The upfront self's mis-truth (about the shadow)	If I don't provide for others first, I'll have no one to lead.
The stretch (when feeling at one's best)	(4) Service to self balances service to others.
The escape route (under stress)	(8) Aggressive and loud preoccupation with advocating other's needs

Zach believed Nick's personal friends owned the fledgling companies. Anxious to share his findings, Zach called me and requested I meet him right away.

When I arrived, Zach pulled me into the conference room and shut the door. I immediately sensed that he was traveling down his escape route to Hot Leader (Type Eight). His gut-laden words provided further proof of where he was operating.

"Nick appears to be out of f***ing control and he has to be stopped. Gillis is being screwed and someone has to take charge here. First, we need to pull in forensic auditors and immediately quarantine all financial records until the audit is complete. Stop all activity except what's needed to keep the shop open. Send most of the employees home on leave, with pay withheld pending each one being cleared of wrongdoing. Put a security guard at the door 24/7 to insure nothing leaves. Bring in an employment attorney to deal with employees' rights. Get a PR person who has crisis management experience in case there is a leak to the media." Zach left no doubt he was intending to heat things up and get me moving IMMEDIATELY.

I paused for a moment to take in the full implications of what Zach was saying.

"Zach. I hear that you are ticked off on behalf of Gillis. You do understand I am in charge of making the recommendations to both Nick and Gillis and that ultimately Gillis is the only one in charge."

"I know, but it's like no one is in charge. It's f***ing crazy. Who knows what else I'll find if I continue looking. This may be just the beginning."

Although the heat Zach was generating wasn't exactly inappropriate to the situation, I knew the temperature needed to come down a notch in order for us to manage this crisis effectively.

"Hey, I appreciate your concern and urgency. You're right. It's why I picked you for this job. But I'm going to put the brakes on you for the moment because I know Gillis would want to hear about this immediately. His manner of dealing with it will be less strident than yours or mine. Stop right where you are and I'll contact Gillis and his lawyer."

"Tell him he's got to get involved or he's going to lose his shirt!!"

"Zach, I continue to be confident that my decision to bring you aboard was the right one. But I need you to get a handle on your anger lest it affect your objectivity and judgment. You're focused on one strategic response, as if there are no other options here. Why? What's this situation triggering in you?"

This stopped Zach in his tracks. Taking his stretch route to the Cool Connector (Type Four), Zach thought about his own emotional connection to the unfolding events. As a young adult, Zach had watched his own family business suffer as the result of a CFO's fraudulent activities. It had ravaged his parents' marriage and set back that company for several years. Replaying the memory tapes from those years of family turmoil, Zach left for his apartment.

Once home, Zach immersed himself in his emotional associations with white-collar fraud. He called his sister and they spoke at some length about how his family's CFO had impacted their lives. He slept restlessly that night, experiencing the emotions he had felt during that low point in his family's life. The lower functioning aspect of his Cool Connector side found it tempting to remain immersed in those emotions rather than deal with the issues at hand.

However, months before taking on Gillis' project, Zach had participated in one of my leadership workshops. Based on what he learned there, he knew to ask himself certain questions about his stretch and escape Routes. He also realized that important information resided in the feelings he was experiencing about his family's past and his current situation with Gillis' company.

The following morning, as he looked in the bathroom mirror, Zach brought himself back to the present. "I owe it to Gillis to manage my state and my temperature. Gillis didn't hire me to be his personal bodyguard, and he didn't hire me to take over his office. I need to get off my escape Route and connect with my emotions in a more thoughtful way. If I can figure out what part of my family's experience with fraud is bothering me, I can use the information to help Gillis. So, what is it?"

Asking the question sparked the answer, which Zach spoke aloud with a mouthful of toothpaste. "I never cared about the missing money, and neither did my parents. It was the violation of trust that hurt most. It took a long time to feel safe again."

As Zach continued to consciously dig deeper into his emotional experience, he realized that the core value of a family office is commitment to the owner's vision and values. "If I just look for missing money, it won't matter to Gillis," he said to himself. Suddenly Zach knew exactly how to proceed.

He resolved to return to the office immediately to examine the remaining documents with this standard in mind: Look for expenditures in conflict with Gillis' values and vision

After another day's search, Zach found additional evidence of financial decisions that clashed with Gillis' values. Nick had purchased extraordinarily expensive first class airline tickets for his frequent overseas business trips. Gillis always flew coach, preferring to divert the difference to his philanthropic foundation for micro enterprises in third world countries. Someone had charged an expensive luxury car to the business, even though Gillis drove an older economy car. The list went on, and Zach had the smoking gun he sought.

Zach's ability to jump off his escape route and consciously benefit from his travel on his stretch route to Cool Connector (4) enabled him to uncover data that moved Gillis. Learning that his values were being violated, that people in need had gone without due to the overindulgence of members of his staff lit a fire under Gillis. Through due diligence, self-awareness, and strategic management of his own temperature, Zach provided the proof Gillis and his attorney needed to make effective changes within the company. The situation was brought under control and new management was brought into place.

An Example of the Hot Achiever (Type Three)

Like many Hot Achievers, Mishram operates at peak performance whenever he sets a goal. A managing partner in a large law firm, he has already had a full and active morning by the time he arrives at his office.

He rises at 5 A.M. to check his e-mail and read the papers while catching a run on the treadmill in his basement gym. Next on his agenda is time with his two pre-school age children, then a quick breakfast and shower. He confides to me that in spite of his very obvious and deep love for his offspring, he finds it difficult to slow to their speed when sitting on the floor to engage in play. "How many times can you try to put the round peg into the square hole at first, and then with giggles of delight, successfully put the round peg into the round hole?" he asks. He appreciates the time with his children, but guiltily wishes they were old enough to choose interests in something faster paced.

By 8 A.M., Mishram is at the office. He begins every workday by reviewing his goals for the day, his firm's progress against projections for the month and progress towards the firm's five year plan. He also takes stock of the progress he's making toward his personal five-year plan.

When I first met Mishram, his personal five-year plan had two goals seemingly at odds: To bank $5,000,000 in his retirement account and to develop his skills in his hobby, auto racing. His plan was that at five years, and age 47, he would retire from the firm and rethink his commitments. He imagined that he would spend more time with his family and would work in the non-profit or philanthropic sectors. Without realizing it, he was explicitly devising a plan in which he would travel on his stretch route to Hot and Cool Implementer (Type 6) for whom commitment and loyalty to a cause (as compared to goals) are key motivators. But like many Hot Achievers, the addiction to speed, action and money distracted him from planning for such commitments as the date approached. When I pushed him on this, he responded: "I just can't leave this much cash on the table. It's money that I could bank for my family's future."

I asked him "Is it really the cash or the excitement of the constant action? Exactly what would improve in your family's life if you had $10,000,000 rather than $5,000,000 in the bank?"

He answered too quickly (and he knew it), "It's the cash". Admitting to his addiction to action's heat was tough for him. He was clearly most comfortable at the 'speed of business' rather than the speed of 'mere mortals' like you and me. In fact my mortal speed was starting to drive him a little nuts. "Get to the point. What do you think I should be doing?" he asked.

"I have a suggestion: Decide what your cash goal REALLY is, and let's work on getting there as fast as possible."

He agreed, and we scheduled a series of coaching sessions designed to help him achieve his revised goals. The outcome of our meetings was his decision to build the billings of his own team in a unique way (reflecting his shadow Cool Connector). Mishram intended to connect more closely with prospects and clients by sharing his passion for fast automobiles with them and by inviting them to participate in auto racing events. A professional level track driver himself, Mishram conducted instructional days in which he would rent the track for the benefit of his clients, and provide them instruction in performance driving. It was the perfect way to demonstrate his trustworthiness and expertise to them in a fun setting. Not surprisingly, this strategy worked very well for all the most important facets of his life. It provided him more time to enjoy his hobby, share it with others, and dramatically build his already healthy legal practice. The trip on his Stretch Road to commitments rather than goals was postponed three years.

THE HOT ACHIEVER (3)	Core Motivations
The upfront self	"I prove myself by winning and producing."
The shadows' truths	(2,4) "Emotions and needs are a source of energy and truth."
The shadow's question	(2,4) "Can you take into account your own emotions and the needs of others?"
The upfront self's mistruth (about the shadows)	"Emotions and needs are obstacles to be overcome"
The stretch (when feeling at one's best)	(6) "Commitment to the cause and to others is more important than simply producing and winning"
The escape route (Under stress)	(9) "If winning is out of reach, I may as well jump out of the rat race and chill."

The escape route for the Hot Achiever is to the Cool Facilitator (Type Nine), being more in the moment, trusting what will come, and allowing himself to be in his surroundings as they are. It is very rare to observe a Hot Achiever take this route. His initial escape is simply to do more of that to which he is already addicted, thus earning the label of 'workaholic'. If he travels to the less functional side of the Cool Facilitator, it is typically not a conscious choice, but most often initiated by a crisis. Such crises often arise when the Hot Achiever gets overly involved in achieving and forgets to truly take care of himself. Mishram fell into this trap.

Focusing on his plans and goals is probably what caused the momentary 'brain fade' Mishram experienced one day while preparing his car for another zip around the race track. The task required complete concentration, but Mishram was not "there". Leaving the pit area in the vintage racecar he had just restored at considerable expense, he forgot that his tires were not warmed up sufficiently to handle the speed with which he was entering the first turn of the track. The car slid into the retaining wall, incurring very costly damage. Neither Mishram nor his client in the passenger seat was physically injured. However, Mishram's sense of self took a beating. He was stunned that he had made such a simple error, and mortified that his carelessness could have had tragic consequences.

Mishram traveled the escape route to the lower functioning aspects of the Cool Facilitator. After escorting his client back to the clubhouse, and apologizing in no uncertain terms, he went off to a quiet corner and sat, and most uncharacteristically, sat some more. Finally, he had the presence of mind to finish his day's commitments and return home. For several days over the weekend, though, he primarily sat, daydreaming, reading, and watching TV. He felt capable of little else and had no desire to do anything more. This was definitely new to him. When he returned to work after the weekend, he found himself able to function only at a reduced pace. It took another two days before he was back to his usual pace.

The experience taught Mishram to focus and concentrate on the matter at hand, so as not to get ahead of himself. This means making a commitment to being present in the moment rather than focusing on what he will do next. By choosing to be present, Mishram has made a commitment to the healthier version of his escape route as a Cool Facilitator. However, unless Mishram consciously commits himself to something bigger than his bank account and his racing goals (and thus his stretch route), he will have insufficient motivation to focus on his safety and health and most likely will return to his typical behaviors. His first step in the direction of his stretch route has been to publicly commit his racing efforts to raising funds for a community organization close to his own and his wife's hearts.

An Example of a Cool Connector (Type Four)

Camille was a photographer who, like many artists, migrated into graphic design as a career. Over many years, her reputation grew until she had so many freelance assignments that she decided to formally establish her own design studio. Rather than hiring employees, she used her ability to connect with others to develop and manage a wide-reaching network of highly respected vendors. The cool and steady way in which she managed these ad hoc partnerships earned her the loyalty of the far-flung group of professionals.

Managing clients, however, was more challenging to Camille. She often found herself traveling her escape route to Hot and Cool Provider (Type 2). Becoming overly compliant to her clients constantly changing wishes and needs consumed too much of her work day, and drained the creative energy she needed to actually produce the work. Finally, she came up with a classic Cool Connector solution: Camille decided to become her own client. Drawing on her deep well of professional connections including clients, creative partners, and individuals in the public sector, Camille created a series of quarterly guide-books, each one focused on one community. The Chamber of Commerce would provide sponsorship along with advertisers. Town officials and community organizations would provide information about the community, with the understanding that the guides would be distributed to every residence in each community. Camille would design and produce each book. Most importantly, these periodicals would provide an avenue for her first love, photography. She formed a business partnership with two other women to create the publishing company, hired salespeople to sell the ads, and looked forward to being able to concentrate on the creative

THE COOL CONNECTOR	Core Motivations
The Upfront Self	"Emotions direct us to what is most meaningful in the world. I will have the guts to feel my feelings."
The Shadows' Truth	(3,5) "There is more to life than one's own emotional reality."
The Shadows' Question	"Do you have the courage to explore reality objectively and be productive in the world as it is?
The Upfront Self's Mistruth (about the shadow)	I will lose my source of energy and wisdom if I focus on data and productivity rather than emotions.
The Stretch (when feeling at one's best)	(1) "There are times to stand up for principles."
The Escape Route (Under stress)	(2) "Others' needs come before my own."

side of the business, once again.

The Guidebooks were a huge critical success. Camille's cover and inside photos were aesthetically beautiful. She had a real gift for being able to understand what was most essential and compelling about each town that could be shown visually. Writers in each community contributed articles that highlighted individuals whose stories invited the reader to truly connect with what was best and unique about each town. The chambers and advertisers were very enthusiastic about this opportunity to provide such a high quality public service.

The business itself was breaking even from the start, a tribute to the strength of the business concept Camille had created. However, like any start-up, this was a very high stress, long hours business. Under the multiple demands of supervising the creation and production of such a complex product, Camille returned to her escape route to Hot and Cool Provider. She constantly alternated her focus to meet the demands of her partners, fill the needs of her salespeople and to deliver on her promises to the many other stakeholders in the guidebook service she had created. As such, she extended her workday far beyond what was sustainable. All-nighters were not unusual. Finally, exhausted, she turned to me for advice.

"So what is the goal here, anyway?" I asked in one of our meetings.

"I want to make money at work that I truly value."

"Is this it?" I continued.

"I love the product so, yes, this could be it. But we won't be turning a profit until we double the number of books we're producing."

Camille's commitment to providing a service to others was so strong that she did not recognize there weren't enough hours in the day to achieve her goals. She would have to scale up the production department. Furthermore, she had created an organization that required more management than she wanted to personally provide. Her original intention, to spend her time doing visually and strategically creative work, had been left behind, due to the needs of the business.

I pushed her towards her stretch route, the Hot and Cool Perfecter (Type One).

"What's the important principle behind this product and your connection to it?"

"I believe these towns are growing so fast that what is special and vital about each community is being lost, whether it's an historic neighborhood, a community group, or a family business of many generations. I could go on and on."

I heated up the discussion.

"Then do you have the courage to make this project 'go on and on'? You're telling me that the project is very important based on principles that you hold dearly, but is only sustainable if production grows from the six books you do at present to at least twelve. I have to tell you, the organization required to produce twelve guide books will require a level of detail management that will take you away from both your creative artistic work and your creative work at the strategic level. Your over-commitment to service via your Escape Route will eat up all the time you have and more., If you have created a viable business, which simply needs rapid growth, you need to either acquire another business allowing you to work at the strategic level, or prepare this business for a sale. Either way, you need to take a stand on your principles."

Camille took a few days to absorb these recommendations. Her first reaction was to become melancholy about the thought of selling her business and losing the emotional rewards it had already provided in spite of its un-profitability. Once she had resolved those emotions, however, she redoubled and heated up her efforts with her staff and vendors on her current business flow in order to put the business in as profitable a position as possible for a sale.

Serendipitously, a local medium-market daily newspaper was flush with capital for expansion. Its vice president of new ventures called Camille, "I had been working through the initial market evaluation and business plan for guidebooks when I came across your company's. I couldn't create a better product. There's no need to reinvent the wheel, here."

The call resulted in an outright purchase of the business and an on-going consulting contract for Camille with the new owners. When I recently called her to ask about her take on this episode in her business career, she noted "My vision was 10 years early. This would have been a very profitable online business from the start. I didn't have then the business savvy and the comfort level with my stretch route to make a profitable and satisfying go of it."

Example of the Cool Thinker (Type Five)

Like many Cool Thinkers, Byron's path was oriented by his own internal thoughts rather than what others thought or expected. The founder of a successful electronics company, Byron was unique in the hi-tech industry. While most hi-tech start-ups sell out in the first few years, Byron had maintained his profitable business for close to fifteen years at the point that we met. The explanation was simple: A Cool Thinker, Byron was motivated to become expert at each of his undertakings. He never wished to master the process of growing companies in order to cash them out. Byron preferred to use the experience of growing his company as an opportunity to learn how to lead. Also, like many Cool Thinkers, he was publicity-adverse. In fact, Byron was so private, even his closest employees found it difficult to read his intentions. Because the hi-tech industry was rife with quick cash-outs, Byron's employees began wondering about his plans for the future.

Keeping his emotions close to the vest was not a good strategy in this case, but Byron seemed oblivious. Noting an increasing rate of employee turnover, Byron's board of advisors enlisted my help.

Byron and I met several times over the course of a year. By our sixth meeting, the mood at his company had gone from tense to extremely taut. It was time for me to turn up the heat on this Cool Thinker. "Tell me again how you explain yourself to your employees when they try to settle their nerves about the possibility of you selling the business?" I asked Byron.

"I don't. It's not on my mind."

"Well, it's on their minds, and it's costing you quite a bit of cash to entice them to continue to stay when you leave them second-guessing your plans for the business."

"I haven't thought about it much."

I heated things up. "I know. I see you avoiding dealing with that huge elephant that's dancing on the table at every senior team meeting: 'What's Byron going to do?' it's trumpeting. Most of your managers deal with this by getting anxious or keeping their resume up to date, ready to jump at any moment."

"Well, I can't be responsible for their emotions."

"Fine, but both of those reactions distract them from what they're supposed to be completely focused on, the work at hand."

"You think so?"

I heated things further. "You are in denial. You keep yourself from thinking about what is really going on by taking your escape route to the Hot Innovator where you keep yourself distracted by doing what's fun and interesting. Face it, you just made two acquisitions, hired a marketing V.P., and took an extended trip to Europe to visit accounts, all in short order without conferring with either myself or your advisory board. That is unlike you and looks from the outside like a typical out-of-control Founder move. "

Byron was watching me closely. "Are you saying I was wrong to do those things?"

"You haven't paused long enough for me to determine that, but that's not the point. The point is that I think you were driven to go on a shopping spree without your usual analyses because, without realizing it, you have wanted to avoid dealing with your most senior leaders' concerns about their future with this company. You can't stand the interpersonal stuff because it isn't your natural strength and it shows. You've looking impulsive rather than analytic."

We had to stop our meeting at that point. I knew that by questioning the motivation behind several major business moves, I had questioned Byron's leadership judgment. I wasn't sure how he would take it.

It was typical for Byron to take 3 to 5 weeks to digest our conversations. This time was no different. I had no idea what he was doing with the heat I had generated in our last conversation.

The answer came in the fifth week when I received an e-mail from

THE COOL THINKER (5)	Core Motivations
The upfront self	"Bug off: I move at my own pace and act only after I objectively and dispassionately master the data."
The shadows' truth	(4,6) "Connection to my own emotions and to my commitments are equally important as my dispassionate observing."
The shadows' question	"Do you have the courage to get close and experience feelings as worthwhile data?"
The upfront self's misperception (about the shadow)	"Others and the emotions they stir within me sap me of my resources."
The stretch (when feeling at one's best)	(8) "I have the courage to make my way as a bold player in the external world."
The escape route (under stress)	(7) "I'll jump into whatever interests me to take advantage of the opportunity rather than waiting to first observe and analyze."

him. "A reporter from the *Wall Street Journal* will be calling you. She's writing an article about Founders who do not cash out. Her editor thinks people like me are bizarre. They've picked me as the poster child. Tell her whatever you want. I trust your judgment." With this move, typically publicity adverse Byron was traveling on his stretch route to Hot Leader (Type 8). He exhibited bold willingness to show himself and defend what he believed, what he had created and those who had made it possible. In the following months, he pushed himself to articulate his vision for the future of his company. Since then, the length of executive tenures at Byron's company has measurably increased.

Example of a Hot and Cool Implementer (Type Six)

Chet, a Hot (more than Cool) Implementer was the epitome of a loyal and committed military professional. Earning his way through college with a ROTC scholarship, he eagerly completed his several year service commitment and then promptly re-enlisted. His promotions came early and often. He enjoyed both the physical and interpersonal challenges of Army life, and thrived in the military's structured paths toward advancement. He became expert at implementing every direction, tip and piece of advice he could absorb. Chet was comfortable with both following and being a hot leader. The sky seemed the limit by the time he had reached Lt. Colonel.

At times, Chet's commitment to his profession reflected the almost mindless drive of a Hot Achiever (his escape route). He preferred constant action to experiencing the anxiety and doubt that head types, particularly the Implementers, are prone to feel. And so it was without a second thought that he followed orders, no matter how difficult or challenging.

Accordingly, Chet did not blink when he was assigned the command of National Guard troops that were to maintain order outside the 1968 Democratic National Convention in Chicago. It had been a violent year of political protest and civil unrest. Martin Luther King and Bobby Kennedy had been assassinated within a few months of each other. There had been widespread rioting throughout the country after Dr. King's death. In that overheated atmosphere, it's not surprising some of the estimated 10,000 street demonstrators gathered near the convention center met harsh treatment by the nervous Chicago Police. The vivid TV news coverage of the events outside the hall had set off a national debate that now reached onto the floor of the convention that Chet was protecting.

Chet received orders to move his troops into position on the city streets near the convention hall. The troops were to be arrayed in lines directly facing the protestors. Chet ordered his officers to prevent the troops from taking action against the protestors. The goal was to keep the demonstrators far enough from the center so they could not disrupt either the convention inside or the coming and going of delegates outside. All the troops had to do was hold their position. Chet made it clear that under no circumstances were troops to allow themselves to be provoked to act outside of his orders.

It was at this moment that Chet received the order from his commanding officer, "Have the troops load (their M-14 rifles) with live ammunition."

His response was automatic. "Understood. Yes, Sir."

THE HOT AND COOL IMPLEMENTER (6)	Core Motivations
The upfront self	"Reliability, Safety, Loyalty and commitment: Why mess with what works? I will have the guts to see things through."
The shadows 'truth	(5,7) "Look objectively: The glass is usually at least half-full."
The shadows' question	"Do you have the courage to be objective about your pessimism and have faith?"
The upfront self's misperception (about the shadow)	"The glass is half empty."
The stretch (when feeling at one's best)	(9) "I can trust the glass to be at least half full."
The escape route (under stress)	(3) "I will cease worrying about my loyalties and commitments and do whatever is necessary to win."

However, Chet paused and rather than race down his escape route and 'just do it', he pictured (as Implementers are prone to do) the possibilities of what could go wrong. He pictured a young National Guardsman panicking at the sight of what might seem to him like a violent mob approaching. He pictured the soldier being the target of provocative taunting. He pictured National Guardsman firing on unarmed protestors outside the Democratic National Convention.

Chet made a decision. The decision was to take no action. He decided to ignore the order. On that day, he may have saved many lives by refusing to rush down his escape route and act without thinking.

After that dramatic night Chet continued his military career, though without the rapid advances that had previously occurred. He retired early, and chose an interesting path along his stretch route to Cool Facilitator. He returned to school, earned a doctorate in social psychology and set up a practice in mediation. He also took his retirement as an opportunity to serve on the boards of several non-profits. Ironically, Chet later learned that the board chair of one of the non-profits had been present on that fateful day in 1968. She had been among the protestors, as a photographer. Her life was one of those that may have been saved by his leadership decision to face rather than to avoid his anxiety.

Example of a Hot Innovator (Type Seven)

Howard, a Hot Innovator, was not ready to retire when his career at the university medical school had finished its 30-year trajectory. True to his type, he was still full of enthusiasm and ready for something new. Something new presented itself in the executive directorship of a major public health clinic. As he navigated his way through the interview process, Howard and I met several times to discuss the organizational and operational issues confronting him.

This was no simple three-examining room rural clinic. This was the largest employer in the city, which operated from three separate locations, offered a variety of services from dentistry to day surgery, and employed a full gamut of physician specialists, nurse practitioners and RN's, technicians, aids, social workers and psychologists. Although Howard had led organizations in the distant past, none of them were nearly the size of this center. Aside from running such a large operation,

Howard faced the additional challenge of filling the shoes of the clinic's Founder, who was leaving after 12 years running the show. Instead of feeling daunted, Howard was already picturing the numerous opportunities he wanted to create for patients and staff alike. However, I believed Howard had skipped over some essential items.

"So Howard, tell me how the negotiations are going." I asked one evening as he excitedly described his ideas.

"Funny you should ask. It's interesting how the board chair is approaching this. He's a great guy, but a little hard to figure out. Twice now he has, with great urgency, asked me to drive the 40 minutes to his office to discuss the job, then gone silent for a week."

"What's the urgency about?"

"Well, I'm not sure. It's as if he needs me on the job as soon as possible, but then, maybe not."

"Have you asked him what's up?"

"No, I haven't."

That simple answer told me that Howard had traveled along his escape

THE HOT INNOVATOR (7)	Core Motivations
The upfront self	"What's interesting is what's important. I will have the courage to try what's new."
The shadows' truth	(6,8) "Real courage is about making a commitment and drawing a line in the sand".
The shadows' question	"Do you have the courage to stop flitting about and fight for something over the long run?"
The upfront self's mis-truth (about the shadow)	"Safety, consistency and reliability are crutches for those who have no faith in life's abundance."
The stretch (when feeling at one's best)	(5) "Objectivity and wisdom balance chasing the exciting."
The escape route (under stress)	(1) "Spontaneity takes a back seat to perfectionism and 'being good'."

route to the Hot and Cool Perfecter (Type One). This likeable, feisty individual was allowing the chair to call all of the shots and responding initially by complying.

I turned up the heat: "So where is the employment contract?"

"That's a great question. Time for me to ask?"

"Ya think? Or maybe you think it would be impolite to expect one?"

Howard laughed.

When I next spoke with Howard, he was acting befuddled.

"We've been talking money. The chair knows that my financial needs are modest but seemed dismayed at my salary expectations, which are decidedly market competitive. We finally did reach some general agreement and he said he'd have the contract written up with a formal offer. So I'm supposed to begin work in one week. In fact, I've already gone in to work several days because of the fluid situation with the lease for the land for the new building, but I haven't seen the contract."

I egged Howard on. "So you've decided to contribute your services to the Center?"

"What do you think I should do?"

"Be yourself Howard, not the compliant good boy you've become. You're acting like you're not ticked off, but I think you want to wring this guy's neck. He may have good reason for his behavior, but he certainly hasn't made an effort to explain his disrespectful approach to closing the deal. Why are you pulling punches on this one and being so damn nice?"

"I think it's what I do when I'm making a transition. Remember this is my first new job in 30 years."

"Well consider the transition made. You know you're going to take this job, and you're going to be great at it."

Within weeks Howard was fully absorbed in a strikingly complex set of decisions that had awaited his arrival. In short order, he and the existing management team had gained the support of the board to push back on a previously negotiated land lease for a new multi-million dollar center, selected an architect, applied for several large grants, begun the capital campaign and taken care of the usual leadership transition responsibilities and opportunities.

It was obvious to me that Howard was able to handle these complex decisions so well because he had traveled his stretch route to the Cool Thinker. (Type Five) Without the dispassionate analysis characteristic of that type, his usual reliance on intuition and quick assessments would have proved inadequate.

Howard was already on his game and then some by the time the contract arrived. It was for the wrong amount. Again traveling his stretch route, Howard utilized the highest functioning aspects of the Cool Thinker to carefully analyze the data. With this information as backup, he pushed back easily, offering solid arguments that helped him re-establish an acceptable figure.

Example of a Hot Leader (Type Eight)

Sam, a Hot Leader and Executive Vice President at a successful airline, had bought an expensive home on several acres in a newly built neighborhood abutting a golf course. Shortly after moving in, he learned that a town committee was in the midst of planning to construct a sewage treatment plant within half a mile of his house. The

THE HOT LEADER (8)	Core Motivations
The upfront self	"No one is ever going to mess with me again. I'll test your strength to see that you are a worthy ally."
The shadows' truth	(7, 9) "Exploration, optimism and harmony rather than force uncover what's important."
The shadows' question	"Do you have the courage to trust?"
The upfront self's misperception (about the shadows)	"Don't trust: It's dangerous to hesitate or cede control to anyone or anything."
The stretch (at one's best)	(2) "Bold action is used to protect and stand up for others."
The escape route (under stress)	(5) "Withdrawal (I'm taking my ball and going home) replaces bold action."

proposed site for the public works plant had been bought by the municipality thirty-five years prior but had laid wooded and unused awaiting approval of the next wave of funding. As the proposal for completing the project, and thus the plant, began to build momentum among town officials and voters, Sam suddenly began to appear at every hearing or public meeting that might touch, even lightly, on the subject.

Sam wanted no part of the new sewage treatment plant and he was much more than an advocate when he pushed for something. He was a force of nature, a bully who was accustomed to having his way.

To introduce himself, Sam showed up in the middle of an informational meeting on the top floor of the historic commercial building at the center of the neighborhood that would first benefit (or not, depending on your view of this project). This was the first time that most of those in attendance had ever seen Sam.

Leo, the town planner, was in the midst of explaining the scope of the project. He held the rapt attention of the several hundred citizens and town officials who also attended the meeting.

"My research uncovered that the first official declaration on the need for this public sewering was in 1950 by an official study committee as a result of an engineering report. It declared the need a public health emergency. The town moved with due speed in response and the Lake Avenue land was purchased for the sewage plant in 1968."

There was laughter at the comment, though not from everyone.

"It is now over 40 years later and we believe the next step is long overdue." Leo pointed to a map and opened his mouth to continue, "The plant would be located here..." He stopped himself when he saw Sam stand.

Interrupting Leo's presentation, Sam stated, "I have a compelling question for you all, and it's the question that must be answered before we spend any more resources or even public time on this matter."

Everyone strained to catch an unobstructed view of this relatively short, but solidly built newcomer who had the guts to interrupt the meeting. They had no need to strain to hear his words, however.

"Please explain the urgency of this project," Sam boomed. "There must be good reason why it has taken so long to gain momentum, yet gained so little in all this time."

Leo began to respond, but Sam cut him off.

"I'll tell you why this has taken so long." Sam continued. " It's simple. There is no reason why anyone would hang the onus of a sewage plant on a neighborhood like mine for the sake a neighborhood like this." Sam swept his arm in the direction of the historic, but admittedly shopworn, village. He seemed both oblivious and unconcerned that the area he had just denigrated was home to many people in the meeting. Nor was he interested in the fact that the worn neighborhood depended on a well-functioning sewer system for its continued viability and possible revitalization.

A murmur arose from the audience. Although this was my first encounter with Sam, and in this instance I was simply part of the audience, I had no doubt that all assembled were being graced by the presence of a Hot Leader who was just warming up. As someone providing advice to the advocates of the project, I knew that Sam would be a very tough adversary. The question was whether his position was cemented, or open to negotiation. I thought, What's the chance he can take advantage of a good shove (the way that Hot Leader's learn) to his stretch route of Hot and Cool Provider? With all that power packed in that frame, he could be a great bodyguard for this project if we could just convince him of ways it might benefit him or others he cared about. I barely had the time to answer my own question.

Harley, a tall, lean attorney, former military officer and presently Chair of the Town Council arose from his seat in another section of the audience. He was in the full righteous heat of a Hot and Cool Perfecter. He stood on principle and his carefully measured words were clear, crisp and commanding. They left no doubt as to what Sam should do.

"I will not have anyone speak in such a disparaging way about any neighborhood in this town now, or ever again in the future." If anyone had cared to drop the proverbial pin, all would have heard it.

As I watched this fascinating scene unfold, there was no doubt in my mind that Sam would tone down the rhetoric for the moment. Hot Leaders do respond to heat. That was not the lingering question for me, however. Although on the surface, Sam seemed to have appointed himself bodyguard for his neighborhood, certain signs pointed to more selfish motivations. This neighborhood leader sat alone. Many of those against the project did attend the meeting, but they didn't seem connected to Sam, a surefire sign that his leadership was more about himself than the needs of the group.

Over the next several months, Sam appeared at so many meetings of the Board of Health, the Sewer Action Committee, the Planning Board, Town Council meetings, etc. etc. that some residents began to ask if he actually had the time to be otherwise employed. When he arrived at one meeting armed with graphs and charts to illustrate the reasons why he and his neighbors opposed the building of the treatment plant, I suspected he had begun to travel his escape route to Cool Thinker (aka the data junkie). When he arrived at each subsequent meeting with newer, more densely data-filled visual aids, I knew for sure he was on his escape route.

Despite his appearance as the bodyguard (aka Hot & Cool Provider) of his neighborhood, Sam's focus was on himself and how the proposed treatment plant would affect him. Whether the map depicted wind direction from the plant or possible hydrological flow, most of these powerful visual aids used Sam's house as the data point. If he had been operating from his stretch route to Hot & Cool Provider, then he would have used the neighborhood as the focal point, not his own house. I shared my assessment with the proponents of the treatment plant. "The self-focused data that Sam has been bringing to each meeting suggests he is stressed enough to have travelled down his escape route. His motivation will not change to your advantage. It's about him and about control. It's about maintaining the value of his house."

True to my prediction, Sam was relentless. I counseled the proponents to continue their work undaunted. "In the short run," I suggested, "Hot Leaders will win battles, so picking your battles against a Hot Leader like Sam is essential."

Not surprisingly Sam won the first battle. The project lost on the first vote. Sam was jubilant but not lulled. He was already rallying his forces before they had finished applauding the vote count. This pattern persisted over four years. Sam never faltered and he was able to slow the project's progress to a crawl.

Then, as abruptly as he had first entered the fray, Sam disappeared without a trace. His house was sold before anyone even noticed it was for sale. His battle done, he promptly withdrew like a Cool Thinker and was not heard from again. Without Sam's power and determination to control the situation for his own sense of safety, his neighbors slowly came to see the benefits of having a sewage treatment plant in town. Within a few years, the project was approved and construction begun.

An Example of a Cool Facilitator (Type Nine)

I met Brett at a conference several years ago. Fascinated by leadership issues and interpersonal communication, Brett had spent some time examining his long, successful career. As it turns out, Brett was one of the lucky few natural leaders who intuitively managed the states and temperatures of himself and his colleagues. He shared the story of one such occasion with me during our first conversation.

While serving as the Executive Vice President of Operations at a budding hi-tech firm, Brett's task was to expand the company's manufacturing capacity to keep apace with the explosive demand for its products. Under Brett's watch, new facilities mushroomed across the country.

Brett's cool leadership style was a good fit for his occupation, since the expectations of both customers and shareholders provided enough heat to keep everyone focused on what needed doing. His unflappable calm was an attribute in an industry prone to unbridled optimism and hyperbole. This unflappability was challenged during a dramatic meeting between the senior management teams of Brett's company and another high profile hi-tech company.

Walt, the CEO/Founder of Brett's company, and Suzanne, the CEO/Founder of the other corporation, had met on other occasions, and never tried to hide their enmity for one another. Brett was surprised that they were willing to explore the possibility of collaborating,

THE COOL FACILITATOR (9)	Core Motivations
The upfront self	"Trust the process. Harmony beats conflict anytime, losing the contribution of no one along the way"
The shadows' truths	(1,8) "Taking a stand to defend a principle or to get things under control are often more important than harmony."
The shadows' question	"Do you have the courage to speak out and join me in taking a stand... or not?"
The upfront self's misperception (about the shadows)	"Anger and tension caused by bold action are destructive and thus to be avoided."
The stretch (at one's best)	(3) "Being productive and 'a player' in the world is at least as important as maintaining harmony."
The escape route (under stress)	(6) "Stick with what is safely reliable rather than risking going with the flow."

but excited about the opportunity to work with another high-stature team in the industry. This meeting, held in the conference room of Brett's company, was the first time Suzanne and Walt had been willing to discuss working together. By lunchtime, both sides were ready for a break. As Brett's team chatted amiably with Walt, Walt began to openly ridicule his adversary's behavior and the general lack of interpersonal savvy shown by Suzanne's entire team. Brett's colleagues laughed along with their boss. Brett was less prone to join in the fun, as he was preoccupied with imagining the meeting from the perspective of the others' side. The joint meeting was reconvened before Brett could gather his thoughts.

Predictably, little headway was made in the afternoon session. Condescension and disdain lay barely below the surface. Then, without warning, Suzanne exploded in heat. Grabbing an unopened can of soda from the table, she launched it across the table in Walt's direction. The can narrowly missed Walt, and left a deep indentation in the wall behind him. Suzanne and her team stormed out, never to return. Brett's team was shocked and stunned by the physical outburst. True to character, Brett's first thoughts were about down playing the open conflict and making light of it. His boss spoke first:

"I need to go make a pit stop. Be back here in ten."

This gave Brett further time to contemplate. He began to travel down his escape route to the lower functioning aspects of Hot and Cool Implementer (Type Six). He began to ruminate about the implementation challenges that were on his plate: ground-breaking for new plants, late arrivals of machinery, human resources dragging its feet on hiring. The cup was suddenly half full in his eyes. He began to imagine all the opportunities for screw-ups that would sabotage the schedule. As discomforting as this obsessing was, it was strangely enjoyable compared to thinking about the near violence he had just witnessed; however, Brett caught himself, and stopped his daydreaming.

Having traveled this unhelpful and avoidant escape route before, Brett knew from experience that he needed to generate some heat to help his team move past this dramatic meeting. He had witnessed teams become seriously distracted from their goals by various interpersonal dramas and he knew how seductive gossiping about such dramas could be.

Brett pushed himself to focus on helping his team put the bizarre experience behind them. He needed them to remain attentive to their tasks if he was to be successful with his own. He could let no obstacle stand in their way. Travelling on what he later learned to be his stretch route to Hot Achiever (Type Three), Brett asked himself, How can I focus others on the goal, in spite of this dramatic distraction?

In a flash of inspiration, Brett rushed to his office, pulled a large framed photograph of one of his new state-of-the-art manufacturing plants from the wall, and removed the picture. Taking the now-empty frame and some markers with him, he raced back to the conference room, just as the others were reconvening.

"Listen, guys. I need you to sign this so it's immortalized," Brett exclaimed as he hung the empty frame around the impressive dent in the wall. In neat block letters, he wrote above the dent, but within the frame, 'The Day She Who Shall Not Be Named Visited This Room.' Others delightedly signed in markers below the dent. Everyone stood back to admire the now framed addition to the boardroom.

Having artfully grabbed everyone's attention, Brett continued. "The purpose of this meeting was to see if there was an opportunity for collaboration. What I see is that any agreement we might have reached would be so obstructed by the differences in our cultures as to be useless. We'd each spend all our time either being disdainful or pissed off at one another, while we made nice in person. And today we showed that making nice in person wasn't going to be much help."

He continued increasing heat to push the team to action: "We have our goals. They are right on our computers and in our heads. We have been hitting them on schedule for two years now. Our shareholders have learned to expect it and our employees count on it. We're not going to win if we spend so much time thinking. We need to get back to our goals. I, for one, am ready. Is there anything that needs to be said before we do that? I've had enough excitement for one day."

Brett's company went on to become a dominant and sustainable player in its sector.

CHAPTER 18
THE MANDATE OF THE FULLY ENGAGED LEADER

You are a leader, and you don't like meetings. Now you know why. Meetings are a source of frustration for uninformed leaders. Why would you want to repeat the experience of leading or participating in a meeting that you could never be sure would be productive, inspiring, or even interesting? Whether you were in charge or sitting among the attendees, until now, you didn't know how to move yourself and your colleagues into the Engaged Field.

You are not alone. That's why Scott Adams, the creator of Dilbert™, has been able to make an entire brand and business empire by parodying leaders and their meetings.

Adams brings the dissatisfaction people feel about meetings into everyday public discourse. By introducing humor into the conversation, the cartoonist moderates the temperature and unleashes a wave of productive energy. In addition, he inspires strangers to participate in his creative process, by submitting ideas based on their own experiences in business.

It is as if each day, Adams conducts a virtual meeting about leadership issues that are relevant to the estimated million individuals who 'attend'. The agenda is always the same:

⇨ 8:00
By e-mail, participants send Adams examples of leadership behaviors that they find particularly bizarre, frustrating, humiliating or incompetent. In other words, they share examples of over-heated or frozen meetings.

⇨ 8:30 AM

Adams draws a Dilbert™ strip based on the above. Each strip incorporates the cartoonist's signature brand of humor.

⇨ 9:00 AM

Participants read Dilbert™. The humor within the comic strip helps moderate readers' temperature, and brings them into the Engaged Field.

⇨ 9:15

Participants e-mail each other or "gather" in small online groups to discuss the leadership and meeting issues covered in that day's comic strip.

⇨ 9:20AM

Virtual meeting adjourns. Participants return to their work newly energized.

This effective management of meeting temperature is found in an unlikely place, at the tip of an artists' pen.

Note the title of this concluding chapter: "The Mandate of the Fully Engaged Leader."

The mandate is to lead meetings that make a difference. You have probably seen examples of such interactions throughout your life, without being aware of what you were seeing. In retrospect, you can identify those moments by considering a time that you met someone who made a profound difference in your life. These master leaders are scattered through your personal history. You remember these people because they made a lasting difference in your life by stirring you to action in some way. They were able to make a difference because they implicitly knew how to manage the temperature of their interactions with you. It's not just their leadership that would never be the same again. Your life was also forever changed.

Allow me to relate one last story, about such a master leader from my childhood:

I don't remember Rosie's last name, but I can easily remember almost everything else about her. Most of all, I remember the meetings she led.

There is much talk nowadays about the importance of having an 'elevator speech', an explanation of who you are and what you do that can be delivered to a fellow rider in the twelve seconds of an elevator trip. I don't recall Rosie's elevator speech, but I can still see her twelve-second 'elevator meetings'. Of course, she had an advantage, since she was an elevator operator in a busy department store.

I was six years old and at that time elevators were not automated. Every elevator had a knob mounted on a disk that was attached to the wall of the 'car'. To move, someone had to rotate the knob to the left or right to speed, slow, or reverse the direction of the car. Because this technology required careful jockeying of the knob to get the floor of the car safely aligned with each building floor, companies hired people like Rosie to run the elevator full time. As she brought the elevator to a full stop, Rosie simultaneously called out the destination "Mezzanine: Women's foundations, perfumes, and hats."

Operating the elevator was Rosie's management, but not her leadership role. Yes, she managed this mundane task all day long, every day, for many years. However, she was a leader who conducted powerful meetings in twelve seconds or less, many times a day, every day.

I know looking back that her meetings had two intended outcomes:

Children will learn to interact with adults in a respectful yet comfortable and collegial manner. Children will maintain their 'learner's mind', their enthusiastic curiosity about the world around them. On one particular day, I had made several complete trips with Rosie from Housegoods and Fabrics at the basement level to the third floor, where the executive and administrative offices were located.

"So what did you see today?" she asked.

"Well I watched the cashiers." The cashiers worked together in one room where they retrieved payments and register receipts from a snake works of pneumatic tubes originating from every corner of the selling floors.

"What did you see?"

"Some of the money sleds are getting old. They make a different sound coming up the tubes. I guess it has to do with the suction. And they don't snap shut with a loud 'click' like the others do."

"Did you ask anyone about them?"

"Well, no."

"Why not? You know those ladies don't bite."

I didn't say anything, so she pushed me carefully, "So what are you going to do next time you're up there?"

"Ask them."

"Then I'll be interested in hearing what they say, just like you are. Probably by later today?"

I nodded, ready for action.

In twelve seconds, without overheating or chilling the interaction, Rosie had engaged all my energies and driven the agenda toward her desired outcome: she wanted me to take action that would enhance both my learning and my ability to interact with adults. Rosie had my attention; the job was as good as done.

Moments later, we stopped at the third floor. Great Uncle Henry stepped in, all six feet of him. I stepped back into the corner, but he found me, ready to begin his 'meeting'. Holding my hand in his, he enunciated words one by one for me to repeat out loud, emphasizing each word with the index finger of his right hand in my outstretched palm.

"Vas".

I repeated, 'Vas".

"Macht."

"Macht," I parroted.

Rosie watched as I dutifully repeated all the words until I could repeat the entire phrase.

"Vas macht ein klein yiddilah." With an air of satisfaction and a pinch of my cheek, Henry exited the elevator car. All in all, this might have been an impressive twelve-second meeting, if he had effectively managed temperature.

While Rosie's intentions were clear to me and inspired me to take action based on them, Henry's well-intentioned leadership was rote and uninteresting to me, despite his overheated (in the mind of a six-year-old)attempt to reach me by holding my hand. Why do I describe it as ineffective? Without fail, as I endured Henry's ritual, my six-year-old mind was thinking, "This guy's a religious fanatic. Why is he always teaching me the Ten Commandments in the elevator?" The heat caused me to want to flee.

It wasn't until I was studying German in college that I understood what Henry had been trying to tell me all those years. Sitting in class one day, I spontaneously smacked my forehead in a combination of enlightenment and embarrassment when I realized my great uncle had been saying, "So, how's the little Jew doing?"

Not exactly the immortal words of a religious fundamentalist. In "meeting" after "meeting" Great Uncle Henry had simply been trying to connect with me, to see how I was doing, in a humorous and warm way. Talk about conveying the wrong message in a meeting! Neither one of us grasped the other person's intentions.

How different is that from meetings you have attended?

The mandate of the fully engaged leader is to conduct meetings that not only lead to the right course of action, but also secure full commitment toward those actions from those attending. This rarely happens in meetings that operate outside of the Engaged Field of temperature. My interactions with Rosie were as effective as any well-lead meeting I have ever attended. She set such a clear agenda and managed temperature and energy so beautifully that I still treasure her for the energy and leadership she brought to those interactions. By comparison, Henry's leadership, as well-intended as I know it was, was two-dimensional. He operated outside the Engaged Field.

By now, you realize that approaching a meeting as if it's just another routine item scheduled by your assistant is a bad idea and a missed opportunity to lead. Giving a meeting the same amount of preparation as a dentist appointment, and entering the room assuming everyone else will be waiting to show you their stuff is a recipe for failure. You will lose influence, credibility and face, often without knowing it. Whether the meeting is a twelve-second elevator ride, a ten-minute review of schedules, or a two-day board session, each interaction brands your leadership in the minds of others.

Because you've read this book, you know that striding into the meeting room with a crisply worded agenda, flow charts and beautifully crafted Power Points is not the same thing as taking charge of a meeting's energy levels. If you want to be a fully engaged leader, your mandate is to manage your meeting's temperature as effectively as Rosie managed temperature in those twelve seconds.

It matters little whether you have a brief facilitator's contract, or an extended executive's contract. Nor does it matter whether you are by nature hot, cool, or both. What does matter is that you take each meeting seriously as an opportunity to engage each person's head, heart and gut. Anything less is not great leadership.

END NOTE

The Enneagram

My work is inspired, in part, by the Enneagram (meaning 'nine-sided figure') a system for understanding human motivations. No one knows the Enneagram's exact origin. However, at the turn of the 19th century, the Armenian intellectual and mystic Gurdjieff and his 'Seekers After Truth' organized information they had collected about the Enneagram from across Asia Minor and Northern Africa. Oscar Ochazo evolved this knowledge into a personality system involving nine types. Claudio Naranjo expanded on Ochazo's work. The 'Founders' of the modern Enneagram community began their work in the US but have since spread over all hemispheres of the globe. These include Maria Beesing, David Daniels, Helen Palmer, the late Theodore Donson, Andreas Ebert, Kathy Hurley, Patrick O'Leary, Don Riso and Jerry Wagner.

A more recent generation of prominent teachers and authors includes Russ Hudson, Tom Condon, Andrea Isaacs, Ginger Lapid-Bogda, Deborah Ooten, Leonard Carr, Bea Chestnut, Michael Goldberg, Mario Sikora and Elizabeth Wagele among many others.

The studies of these groundbreaking individuals profoundly influenced my work. I owe appreciation to each of them and to my colleagues in the International Enneagram Association, with whom I have had the honor of learning and sharing information on what makes leaders and meetings tick.

ABOUT THE AUTHOR

Bart Wendell, Ph.D. is a business consultant and psychologist. As a master facilitator and trusted adviser, his clients have included The International Monetary Fund, PBS, NPR, The Corporation for Public Broadcasting, Massachusetts General Hospital, Fidelity Investments, The Ford Foundation, The United States Air Force Academy, and RockTenn.

In addition to his consulting practice, Bart has served on the adjunct faculty of the Massachusetts School of Professional Psychology and as a seminar leader at Harvard Business School's Advanced Management Program. He has made guest appearances on CNBC Television's "On the Job" and WNBC's nationally syndicated show, "Small Business Report."

He serves on the board of the nationally-recognized Francis W. Parker Charter Essential School and The Massachusetts Moderators Association. He is past Vice President of The International Enneagram Association.

Bart received his B.A. and M.A.T. from Wesleyan University and his Ph.D. in Psychology and Organizational Development from Duke University. He holds a Licensure in Psychology in Massachusetts.

Additional information including a blog is available at www.WendellLeadership.com.

Bart can be reached at bwendell@WendellLeadership.com.

Made in the USA
Charleston, SC
09 November 2010